50
SUCCESSFUL
HARVARD
APPLICATION
ESSAYS
FOURTH EDITION

Also Compiled and Edited by the Staff of *The Harvard Crimson*

55 Successful Harvard Law School Application Essays,
First & Second Edition

50 SUCCESSFUL HARVARD APPLICATION ESSAYS

FOURTH EDITION

With Analysis by the Staff of *The Harvard Crimson*

 ST. MARTIN'S GRIFFIN ✷ NEW YORK

www.stmartins.com

Library of Congress Cataloging-in-Publication Data

50 successful Harvard application essays : what worked for them can help you get into the college of your choice.—Fourth edition.
    pp. cm.
  ISBN 978-1-250-04805-9 (trade paperback)
  ISBN 978-1-4668-4834-4 (e-book)
  1. College applications—Massachusetts—Boston.   2. Harvard University—Admission.   3. Exposition (Rhetoric)   I. Harvard crimson.   II. Title: Fifty successful Harvard application essays.
  LB2351.52.U6A13 2014
  378.1'616—dc23

                                                                    2014008532

St. Martin's Griffin books may be purchased for educational, business, or promotional use. For information on bulk purchases, please contact Macmillan Corporate and Premium Sales Department at 1-800-221-7945, extension 5442, or write specialmarkets@macmillan.com.

First Edition: July 2014

10   9   8   7   6   5   4   3   2   1

CONTENTS

Contents

IV. Overcoming Obstacles

V. Foreign Life

VI. Passion

VII. Inspiration

Contents

VIII. EXPERIENCES

ACKNOWLEDGMENTS

The Harvard Crimson would like to thank the members of the team who crafted this book and made it successful. We are most grateful to the essay writers who were willing to submit their work for public scrutiny—this book is only possible because of your generosity. Next, to our essay reviewers, whose many collective hours of work were integral to this book's publication. The members of staff of *The Crimson* who put this project together deserve a thank-you: Maya Jonas-Silver and David Liu, who led the charge on this project, and Andrew Creamer, LuShuang Xu, Nikita Iyer, Samir Gupta, John Finnegan, Jessica Li, Maliza Namude, Patrick Liu, Caden Broussard, Bobby Samuels, and Joseph Botors, who provided the support necessary to complete it. And of course, without Matt Martz, our editor at St. Martin's, none of this could have happened—thanks so much, Matt, for everything.

I. INTRODUCTION

The Admissions Essay

You spend four years working on your GPA and four hours sitting for the SATs and now you're left with one last big obstacle—the college application essay. Now you're sitting at your desk, staring at a blank computer screen, wondering how someone like you will ever find anything worth writing about. If that sounds familiar, read on.

Before getting unduly stressed, remember this: When you express yourself in an application essay, you can attempt to sum up all that you are, but you won't succeed. No one fits into five hundred words. If, in that space, you can successfully present even one fragment of who you are, you've done your job.

Some people write essays about their experiences—about travel abroad or new people they've met or new things they've learned. Sometimes, people take those experiences and use them to explain the way they've lived their lives or hope to live their lives in the future. And when these options fail, applicants turn inward, to their own thoughts on, really, anything.

Every type of essay has its advantages. Writing about experiences gives the reader an engaging story to follow. Looking forward with an application essay is a good route for someone who feels like there is more to say about the future than about the past. And writing an introverted essay requires nothing more than an open mind.

So don't despair—for everyone, there is an appropriate topic for the personal statement.

Remember the primary intention of the personal statement: Give your readers a sense of who you are as a person. This is the part of your application in which you get to communicate directly with the decision-makers, and you want to leave them with the impression that you are a full, interesting individual with something to add to their college.

The second purpose of the personal statement: Readers will look over these statements as one of very few writing samples submitted to them. For great writers, this makes the personal statement a perfect opportunity to highlight a talent for self-expression. But a borderline application could be pushed off the edge by incorrect spelling or grammar or awkward word use or sentence structure. This part of the personal statement is not hard, so get it right. Have anyone and everyone who is willing to proofread your essay do just that.

Third, these essays allow the readers to put emotions and agency behind the list of accomplishments they see on a résumé. Do not list your résumé in your application—they already have that information. Use the essay to humanize one or, at most, two of the activities listed. Seeing that you were the captain of your high school volleyball team doesn't tell admissions officers the same thing they learn after reading an impassioned description of what leadership means to you, in the context of high school volleyball. But be careful—in this instance, the important part of the essay *must be* your interest and passion for leadership and not the fact that you were a leader. If you are writing about the captainship of your volleyball team because it is impressive and not because you are passionate about it, you need to rethink your approach.

Now that you have a sense for what a personal statement is, we have compiled our top tips for a successful writing process.

1. Start brainstorming early. If you start early enough, you'll give yourself time to consider ideas, mull them over, and then reject them. Attempting a late start will lead to problematic results— giving yourself the time to throw out an essay or two is key to submitting your best possible work.

2. Find something interesting and original to write about. If your essay is indistinguishable from the fifty other applicants who also visited the Grand Canyon and were struck by the magnitude of it, you will not leave an impression with the admissions

officer you are trying to impress. No need to find something outlandish, but try to avoid writing about common experiences in a predictable way.

3. Use the people around you to test your idea. Talk to your friends, parents, and teachers before you start writing. If they seem uninterested, that's a pretty good sign that you should try something else. And remember, people are not always as critical as you need them to be. Look for enthusiasm, not just positive feedback, before you settle on a topic.

4. Sometimes, the hardest part about drafting an essay is getting started. If you've found a topic but don't know how to put it onto paper, try to just start writing. Maybe you feel like you're opening in the middle; maybe you're just scribbling sentences onto a whiteboard. Whatever gets you to move from thinking to writing will be helpful.

5. Cut and discard. If something isn't working, don't be afraid to drop it and try something else.

6. Grab the reader at the beginning, hold on to him through the middle, and leave him satisfied at the end. If your essay starts dragging, you'll lose the reader. If your introduction is boring, you'll never get the reader's attention. And if your conclusion is disappointing, you'll leave your reader with a bad last impression. Avoid all of these things. Write a good essay all the way through.

7. Avoid overreaching. Essays that try to do too much in five hundred words read exactly as such. Don't let yours fall into this trap. The word limit for these is set because that's the scale the

admissions office wants you thinking on. You are not solving the world's problems with these essays, nor are you writing a great work of literature. You are just giving the reader a taste of who you are.

8. Every good essay has a point, whether you planned for it to or not. Figure out what it is and stay focused. To get your message across, you can't waste time with distractions. You need to be working toward the ultimate message in every line.

9. This one is predictable: Proofread. Get all the input you can. Don't agree with all of it and don't do what everyone says, but get a range of opinions. If one person loves your essay and another forty-nine don't get it, you've only got a 2 percent chance of finding an admissions officer who will appreciate you. Keep your odds in mind—stand by your beliefs, but not to the point of foolishness.

10. Be yourself. The worst thing you can do is present someone other than yourself. And an essay that reads as hyperbolic or fake will not make a good impression.

So go forth and compose. And remember that what we said in tip number 10 goes for this book as well—listen to what we say, and then make your own decisions. For the essay to be truly successful, who you are needs to come through—your hopes and dreams, your insights and accomplishments. Getting feedback is important, but the applicant you present through this essay is unique. Ultimately, the only person who can write your personal statement is you.

Good luck!

II. IDENTITY

The way you identify yourself is a powerful part of who you are, and if you have strong feelings about your identity, those can be described in an impactful, descriptive essay. In addition to creating an easy platform from which you can talk about yourself, an essay on your identity is a good way to demonstrate that you give careful consideration to who you are. While identity is intrinsic, it can also be taken for granted; putting real thought into your identity and expressing it in a personal essay is indicative of the way you approach the rest of your life—thoughtfully and insightfully.

But essays on identity can easily become overly cerebral. Most people have a complex identity inspired by many different things. Attempting to explain all of these will almost certainly prevent you from adequately explaining any of it sufficiently. The essays that are most effective take a direct view of identity—maybe just attempting to explain one part of an identity—and focus on that. In a five-hundred-word personal statement no reader expects you to fully explain the whole of you. When writing essays about identity, choose one part of who you are and focus on that.

Caden B.

I have blond hair and pale skin. On the color wheel, my father is a rich mocha, my sister is a warm copper, and my mother is a perfectly tanned caramel; I am somewhere between cream and eggshell on the opposite end of the spectrum. Being stereotypically white can be difficult when you're African American.

The beginning of high school was when I first began to feel that my fair complexion hid my true identity. When I entered ninth grade, I was delighted to find myself in the company of an entirely new group of friends. Upon meeting my parents for the first time, my friends smiled warmly at my mother and gaped at my father, their eyes widening as they flitted between him and myself. However, I was pleased to find that all of them were accepting of my family's ethnic composition. As our group became closer, we often discussed our futures. During one conversation, we outlined our weddings, collapsing into fits of giggles upon hearing each other's extravagant dreams. Once our laughter had subsided, one girl said more seriously, "One thing's for sure, I could never marry a black guy. It would just be too difficult with the race thing." I blinked, waiting for a reaction. None came. Why had no one jumped to my defense? Did people not see my white mother and my black father when they looked at me? It was then that I realized to my friends, I wasn't black.

Incidents like this made me recognize that being biracial has inherently given me perspective that many people lack. When a friend told me that her parents would never allow her to date someone of a different race, I couldn't understand why. When I revealed my biracial heritage to a black friend, she became noticeably warmer toward me and happily shared the news with her friends as we walked by them in the hall. My much darker sister does not share these experiences. We draw from the exact same gene pool, but my sister's complexion allows her complete racial inheritance to shine while mine cloaks half of it.

My sister knows her race because her appearance reflects it. But do I? Is a girl still black if nobody sees it? Should it matter? Growing up pale, blond, and black has influenced me. I feel obligated to immediately tell people about my race because my looks do not convey it. Nevertheless, I know who I am. Though my friends joke about me skipping the "black gene," I am just as connected to my father's Louisiana roots as I am to my mother's Alabaman ancestors. Racial identity is marked by more than arbitrary features like skin tone, and while we are unable to choose our exact coloring, we do choose who we are. My appearance and the responses it elicits have shaped me but do not control me. Beneath fair hair and light skin, I see a girl who is both black and white. I see me.

REVIEW

At first glance, Caden's essay seems like a generic essay about "diversity"—a hot college-acceptance buzzword. Wrong. Caden takes the important topic of identity and weaves it into a beautifully composed coming-of-age tale, showing how her self-confidence and ability to overcome challenges grew. She writes in a playful tone that makes reading her essay an entertaining experience rather than a chore. By incorporating memories of conversations with friends in her freshman year in high school, she lets readers into her personal life, taking the edge off the serious undertones of her conflicts with "extravagant dreams [of weddings]." This combination of her racial identity issues and her youthful memories shows a maturity of thought and understanding of others as well as herself.

However, she does not forget to draw the attention back to the key point of her story—her firm acceptance of her character. After her first two sprightly paragraphs, her tone shifts and becomes authoritative. She employs short and straightforward sentences as the essay progresses, such as the declaration: "I know who I am" in the final paragraph. Caden writes with a powerful voice that distinctly proves she accepts her biracial identity, despite her appearance that leads others to make false assumptions. Although the final line, "I see me," can be seen as a reach, it works for Caden. By that point in the essay, she has earned it. It caps off the confident tone of the last few paragraphs that express her comfort with her racial identity. All in all, Caden created a well-written story that displays both her writing prowess through smooth transitions between different voices and her ability to overcome the greatest challenge of being comfortable in one's skin.

—Jiho Kang

CHRISTIANE ZHANG

American food is the pot on the backburner that I check only occasionally. Eleven years of living in the United States have attuned my taste buds to the marbled texture of ground beef alongside melted American cheese, topped off with a refreshing, crunchy layer of lettuce, complemented by the sweet contrast of ketchup, all sandwiched within an unremarkable bun. Somehow I find myself enjoying this greasy, messy, yet satisfying meal; the chance (fatty) bacon strips only increase the appeal of my burger. Indeed, in my family, I am the only one who appreciates its savor and simplicity. But I know I could not survive on a diet of burgers, fries, hot dogs, chocolate chip cookies, or any food that I brand as "American," as enticing as they sometimes are. Instead, the two thousand (or more likely four thousand) calories that I take in every day originate eight thousand miles away.

At home, Mom is the chef, and in my fair and equitable opinion, no one rivals her in traditional Chinese food. Her signature dish is *qiongrenmian*, literally "poor man's pasta," which I would voluntarily eat every day, unlike its American counterparts. More of a stew, *qiongrenmian* comprises of clumps of flour and water, boiled into small, soft bites floating along with tender pieces of pork, splashes of tomatoes, and dispersed clouds of eggs. The flavors meld together, and so I add some sweet chili garlic sauce, the playfully piquant surprise offsetting the cozy, home sensation. My taste buds are so responsive that I wonder if I am not perhaps a poor Chinese man, as the dish's name suggests. Thankfully, I have yet to see a poor man in China enjoy something this luxuriously poor, this deliciously simple, so I'm reasonably certain that I am not a Chinese beggar.

As much as I love simplicity in cooking, I cannot resist the more complex wonders of *la cuisine française*, and I will frequently indulge in my love of French baking. Perhaps I romanticize my French birth a little. Regardless, I feel decidedly French as I watch my raspberry *soufflés* rise or my *biscuit aux pommes* turn golden. My most recent escapade involved five hours of preparation to produce fragile, miniature white *macarons* filled with smooth chocolate *ganache*. Despite the tedious work, French desserts seem incapable of disappointing, whether after an elegant meal of savory *steak tartare* and *andouille* sausage, or simply a burger or *qiongrenmian*.

My next project? I think I'll catch a Canadian goose and make some *foie gras*.

REVIEW

The writer's essay describes herself in terms of cooking—she is one of many identities with the drive to discover new ones. By introducing herself not directly as a multicultural person, she piques our interest in her varied heritage. Additionally, by mentioning her "next project," whether in jest or seriousness, the writer hints at her willingness to go ahead and try new things, to take on new goals. The essay is a display of subtle hints at a person through the revelations of food.

However, the immediacy with which she dives into food and the total separation of her nonfoodie self leaves a very focused view of who she is. Though the overall effect of an essay that sounds like it could appear in *Bon Appétit* is tempered by a personal writing style,

dotted with parentheticals and soft humor, the overall feel of large por-
tions of the essay is decidedly not personal nor revealing. With a little
less detail, particularly in the next-to-last, French-laden paragraph, the
writer could have preserved the intimacy of revealing her tastes and
culture in a subtle way.

But overall, the essay presents a likable, thoughtful person with a
strong sense of who she is. Christiane succeeds at expressing herself
as a bicultural individual with a taste for good cooking.

—Sara Kantor

WHITNEY GAO

It is October 9, and a multitude of high school students have gathered at the test center for a morning of standardized testing. This morning, we are all faceless little numbers. This morning, I am registration number *******7. It is very nice to meet you.

Three hours later, it is time to commence a mass exodus. A sea of bodies floods the halls before bursting through the floodgates, eventually separating and becoming individual trickles. As we all return to our various corners of Little Rock, we finally lose the anonymous masks and become individuals. I am no longer just a number; I am now me.

I am a sister. I am a daughter.

I am an under-the-covers reader of fashion magazines. I am absolutely obsessed with math and science. I am the girl whose laugh you hear all the way down the hallway.

I am a figure skater whose favorite spin is a layback. The ice rink is my escape, and the Diamond Edge Figure Skating Club is a second family. I am a pianist whose favorite piece is Edvard Grieg's Piano Concerto in A Minor, Op. 16. My thirteen-year-long love affair with music has led me to much happiness and accomplishment, and I hope it continues for all of my life. Endless hours devoted to these activities have taught me skills necessary for the future, including self-discipline and perseverance.

I am an ardent volunteer in my community, and I have the privilege of serving as the president of the largest Junior Civitan club in the world. The people I have met and the experiences I have had have left lasting impacts on me and given me memories and lessons that I will carry forever. Being a Civitan, while allowing me to participate in something that I love, has taught me the gift of appreciation. In one particular experience, I was especially struck with the amount of good fortune I possess. While working with the Salvation Army during their Christmas Angel Tree program, I met a mother whose family had become homeless very recently after a fire burned their house to the ground. The past few days had been an unimaginable struggle for hope. At the end of her story, her eyes were not the only ones filled with tears. Her unceasing thanks over just a few clothes and toys for her children brought my world into perspective for me. Since then, I have become the most avid promoter of community service because I believe that it is unquestionably essential to give back to the community in which you have thrived.

Numbers will always follow me. About two weeks later, I would be 2400. In the spring, a smattering of 5s would label me as well. But at the end of the day, the numbers and academics all fall away, and I am just me. The only number that remains is 1; there is only one me.

I am Whitney, and it is very nice to meet you.

REVIEW

This essay creates an image of a well-rounded girl; disciplined and dedicated, passionate about her extracurriculars, and academically excellent. She writes in smooth prose and demonstrates that she has put thought into who she is while drafting this personal statement.

But Whitney falls short in her attempt to escape anonymity and to stand out of the crowd of "faceless little numbers." This personal statement reads like an enumeration of accomplishments with little or no analysis. Whitney writes that math and science are her obsession, but she does not sound truly passionate and academically motivated;

she writes she is an accomplished pianist, but she does not explain how playing makes her so happy. While it is clear that the applicant has numerous talents, the superficiality with which these talents are treated makes this essay overall unimpressive.

Although she does not wish to be defined by numbers, Whitney hints at her perfect SAT and AP scores, which not only contradicts her stated purpose but is also inappropriate, as those numbers are already well in evidence in other parts of the college application. The one passage where simple listing turns into a more complex analysis of the applicant's extracurricular involvement is the description of her service at the Junior Civitan club. Had the experience at the Christmas Angel Tree program taken an even more central stage, Whitney would have been more successful in leaving the sphere of anonymity. Similarly, a deeper analysis of the "self-discipline" and "perseverance" that ice-skating and music taught her would have given the reader a better insight into the applicant's personality.

Whitney has put together all the pieces of a successful college application essay, but fell into a common trap—she tried to explain all the great things about herself, and while attempting to do that failed to stand out. If she focused on one of these many accomplishments, Whitney would have gone from a good and ultimately successful essay to a truly great one.

—Francesca Annicchiarico

Chaffee Duckers

I think the most tragic part of my childhood originated from my sheer inability to find anything engraved with my name. I never had a CHAFFEE license plate on my hand-me-down red Schwinn. No one ever gave me a key chain or coffee mug with the beautiful loops of those double Fs and Es. Alas, I was destined to search through the names; longingly staring at the space between CHAD and CHARLOTTE hoping one day a miracle would occur. Fortunately, this is one of the few negative aspects of a name like "Chaffee Duckers."

My name has always been an integral part of my identity. Sure, it sounds a bit like my parents created it from a bag of Scrabble tiles, but it comes from a long-lost ancestor, Comfort Chaffee. Now it's all mine. In my opinion, a name can make or break a person. The ability to embody a name depends on the individual. My greatest goal in life is to be the kind of unique person deserving of a name so utterly random and absurd.

I began my journey in preschool. Nothing about me screamed normal. I was not prim, proper, and poised. I preferred sneaking away from my preschool classroom, barefoot, in the purple velvet dress I wore every single day to resting obediently during nap time.

I grew up in a family akin to a modified *Brady Bunch*. Stepsisters, half sisters, stepbrothers, and stepparents joined my previously miniscule household. But in a family of plain names like Chris, Bill, John, Liz, Katherine, and Mark, I was still the only *Chaffee*.

I was a bit of a reverse black sheep in my family. My name helped me carve an identity separate from my myriad of siblings. Instead of enriching my brain with *Grand Theft Auto,* I preferred begging my parents to take me to the bookstore. While my parents mandated homework time for my brothers, they never questioned my work ethic or wiretapped my assignment notebook. The thing that set me apart from the herd was that I was self-disciplined enough to take control of my own life. From the very beginning I never depended on my parents' help or motivation to finish my schoolwork. Putting school first came naturally to me, much to the distaste and confusion of my siblings. My work ethic became known as the patented "Chaffee Method."

As I got older, I began to embody my name more and more. I didn't want to be that girl with the weird name in the back of the class eating her hair, so I learned how to project my ideas in both written and spoken forms. I was often picked to lead classroom discussions and my complete disregard for making a fool of myself bolstered that skill. The manner in which I operate academically is perfectly described as *Chaffee*-esque; including but not limited to elaborate study songs, complex pneumonic devices, study forts, and the occasional John C. Calhoun costume.

I take pride in the confusion on a person's face when they first read my name. Seeing someone struggle over those two unfamiliar syllables fills me with glee. I feel as though I am adding a new word to their vocabulary. So on my last day as a page in the U.S. Senate, I prepared myself for the anticipated awkward stumbling as Senator Harry Reid thanked me by name in his closing address. But the stumble never came. I felt very humbled by his perfect pronunciation. Perhaps *Chaffee* is actually catching on!

REVIEW

Chaffee's essay is strong because it follows a clear narrative, all enabled by her rather unusual name. While not everyone has a name as unique as "Chaffee," and are therefore unable to use this approach, writing an essay about an experience or aspect of one's life that is singular to oneself is a smart approach for any college essay. She shapes her development from preschool to high school in the lens of her name, demonstrating the importance that it has played throughout her life.

Chaffee's initial anecdote immediately grips the reader; many people have shared the experience of looking for engraved merchandise, and the fact that she can find none bearing her name sets the stage for the rest of the essay. Chaffee quickly qualifies her discontent with her name, stating that this anecdote "is one of the few negative aspects of a name like 'Chaffee Duckers.'" Unfortunately this qualification is a bit misplaced since she immediately returns to tell a story of her upbringing while failing to address any of the positive aspects of her name until paragraphs later. This is a bit of hedging that isn't entirely necessary in the limited space allowed by most personal statements.

Yet, the essay works quite well. Chaffee spends a great deal of time elaborating on how she was different from both her family and others with examples of her transgressions in preschool and her penchant for schoolwork and education as opposed to procrastination or video games like *Grand Theft Auto*. Chaffee toots her own horn just a little bit when describing the merits of her work ethic, but it is still fairly endearing overall, and there is no shame in sharing a desire for learning. Chaffee states in the conclusion of her essay that she now takes "pride in the confusion on a person's face," as they try to read her name, demonstrating how she has now accepted and come to appreciate the fact that she does not share a name with the average Mary, Dick, or Jane.

—David W. Kaufman

JONATHAN PALMER SMITH
Cooks vs. Chefs

I could sense my mom's eyes rolling when Paula Deen erupted into her signature cackle on the television. Throughout the summer, as I deteriorated in insoluble boredom, the Food Network had become my atrophic channel of choice. With her creamy Southern drawl and not-so-subtle use of every English teacher's worst nightmare, "Y'all," I reveled in her thirty minutes of butter, batter, and calories. However, Paula Deen was not the only Food Network star who I enjoyed watching. In fact, Ina Garten (aka Barefoot Contessa), a person whom I could just picture convulsing at the thought of Ms. Deen's fried ice cream, also provided me with the entertainment I so desperately craved. Countering Paula's folksy phrases, she preached the importance of "good kosher salt" and gushed about how coffee so elegantly elicits the richness of cocoa before prancing away to the local market.

However, the contrast between these two celebrity chefs highlights an even greater divide in society—the culinary smackdown of cooks versus chefs. The former emphasizes practicality, exudes warmth, and occasionally throws all nutritional guidelines to the wind. They idolize "short cuts," and don't need a tablescape to create an ambience befitting of their down-home cookin'. The chef, conversely, sneers at the desecration of carefully guarded culinary techniques. What happened to slow-roasting that chicken for eight hours? Must the rabble persist in mispronouncing "Worcestershire"? And why must everything they say taint the palate? While bemoaning these pesky tendencies, the Contessa carefully folds her chocolate mousse until it reaches the perfect consistency—coddling it like you or I would a child. Chefs allude to their gustatory odysseys in the south of France or on the islands floating in the Mediterranean much like those perfectly crisped crou- tons dancing upon the surface of a velvety tomato-basil soup laced with just a touch of Fino. Practicality is not of the essence, for the emphasis rests on process and design.

Yet, the chasm between these two culinary factions extends far beyond the set of *The Next Food Network Star*. College represents a chance to broaden one's intellect and, more importantly, appreciate the myriad perspectives of our society. But what is learning without prac- tical implications? To abscond to an Ivory Tower for a lifetime is to withhold knowledge that could alter the world. The chefs deserve some credit for their worship of technique, but does a perfect process necessarily yield a superior result? In all seriousness, Paula and Ina shed light on my collegiate goals. I want to learn something practical— something that might actually help to change the world. Because, maybe, just maybe, one person can make a difference—not a big dif- ference: but a difference nonetheless. Regardless of where I eventually attend, my pragmatism will drive me to embrace the real-world impli- cations of all that I learn. And as I sit in my dorm room, typing out the last words of a thesis, Paula Deen's cackle in the background will remind me of how right those cooks might actually be.

REVIEW

Jonathan strikes a commendable balance between storytelling and the insights gleaned through introspection. His statement prominently features charismatic and familiar characters. By using a candid approach, the author establishes a sense of security and elicits an investment from the reader. Though he accomplishes much within a limited space, Jonathan places himself in a position that may undermine the purpose of a personal statement: to reveal motivations, desires, and the inner conscience of an applicant not otherwise apparent.

As he continues, Jonathan ventures further into a foreign territory. While his commentary on cooks versus chefs illustrates the author's command of academic analyses, the piece thus far says little about him. Descriptions of culinary technique and delicious dishes leave an impression on the senses. Coddling chocolate mousse like a child and venturing on gustatory odysseys for velvety tomato-basil soup is certainly unique. Neither memorability nor entertainment value are of concern. These components are frequently most difficult to incorporate, yet Jonathan demonstrates clear mastery. However, even two-thirds through his piece, Jonathan continues telling a seemingly irrelevant story and leaves the reader at a loss in regards to his ultimate ambition.

Finally, as the third paragraph begins, the author reveals the purpose of his prose. The remainder of the story serves as a scaffold to demonstrate a commitment to broadening one's intellect. Furthermore, he conveys a maturity that allows him to extract profound meaning from a seemingly banal sequence of events. Jonathan finds his greatest strength as he seamlessly bookends his piece. Drawing a parallel between Paula Deen and collegiate goals is indeed a difficult task. But perhaps it is this improbability of success that makes Jonathan's essay compelling.

—Fatima Mirza

SARA PRICE

Bands of Experience

The fabric that constitutes my life is a fusion of multitudinous hues and textures, shut away in a box under my bed only to be retrieved in preparation for each day. My personality is best conveyed through these minute fragments of my existence, manifested in a headband collection.

I have been accumulating decorative headgear for over a decade, and have built an assortment nearly three hundred strong. The array includes massive, miniscule, plastic, and cloth, with a span of colors far exceeding the range of the rainbow. Such variation exists because each headband encapsulates my identity on a given day. Thus, the story of my life is unearthed every morning when I unfasten this uncanny box of memories.

Today, in the midst of burrowing for the perfect topper to my tresses, I encounter the glossy white headband that was once a versatile staple of my adolescent wardrobe. As I caress its smooth ivory surface, I instantaneously feel the fleeting freedom of childhood I once experienced as it cradled my cranium. The girl who wore this accessory was boundlessly charismatic and endlessly expressive, an intrinsic actress lacking the proper stage. I was but a young teenager unable to afford drama camp or acting lessons, dreaming of one day shining in the spotlight.

Amid my reminiscing I come across a soft burgundy headband perfectly matching my corresponding uniform polo, which I donned on the intended date of my inaugural high school play audition. Although in my eager anticipation I felt my act was as coordinated as my outfit, my sophomoric self was in for a shock. Laryngitis paralyzed my voice that fateful morning, and I had to hoarsely mouth an explanation to the drama director in disappointment. Generously, he gave me a small part regardless because he knew of my unremitting work ethic. Determined to grasp that chance by exceeding his expectations for excellence, I invested my entire emotional energy into a comedic improvisational exercise at my first practice. After a short bout of speechlessness, the drama club burst into an amalgamation of applause and laughter. Finally, my routine began to emerge from behind the curtain.

Soon the faint shimmering of glitter jolts my musing forward as I recall the evening I displayed a certain purple headband as a costume component. It augmented my guise as the Enchantress, the first of three roles I played in *Beauty and the Beast*. Over a year had passed since my ill-fated audition, and at last all eyes focused as me as I opened the show with a brief self-choreographed routine. I basked in the exhilarating joy of acting, enhanced by my renewed understanding of the immense resolve required to seize the stage. My headbands accompanied me through the entire journey, and thus they are of great personal value.

It seems peculiar that the most precious artifacts I possess sell for approximately $1 each. Yet these bands are my treasures, as they hold my past experiences while stretching to encompass the performances held in my future.

REVIEW

Sara adopts a unique and innovative approach to her essay; instead of speaking directly about her love of theater, she presents this passion through the framework of her headband collection. This narrative structure gives her an avenue to exhibit the multifaceted nature of her personality, which she describes to be as varied as her array of headbands.

Throughout her essay, Sara reveals herself to be capable of highly evocative imagery that successfully skirts oversentimentality. There are a few aspects of her essay that can be improved, however. First, her headbands are given a large amount of credit in the first two paragraphs—it is too much to say that "the story of [her] life is unearthed every morning" when she puts on her headgear.

Additionally, much of the language in the essay is overwritten. Using more subdued language to express the significance of her headbands would convey the same message while maintaining credibility. Her word choice is excessive—her use of words like "multitudinous," "minute," "donned," "unremitting," and "amalgamation" is at best unnecessary and at worst misleading.

With all of that said the last paragraph of the essay is quite commendable: The line on the $1 monetary value of her headbands is very memorable and, the final sentence ties all parts of the essay together, providing a highly effective conclusion for what is ultimately a deeply personal and revealing essay.

—Melody Y. Guan

Michelle Choi

"You should scrub off the top layer of your skin whenever you lose a round," my debate teammate once advised me.

"That's not practical," I replied.

"Neither is your refusal to wear clothes you've lost important debate rounds in. Your wardrobe has *very* little to do with your success."

Half of me disagrees with him. I still bring three BIC Round Stic pencils with 0.7 lead to every test because my gut tells me this fastidious procedure raises my scores. I'm still convinced that labs receive better grades if written in Calibri. And I still won't rewear clothes in which I've lost crucial rounds.

Yet the other half of me is equally dismissive of my own superstitions. I love logic, never failing to check that steps in a proof lead to a precise conclusion without gaps in reasoning. Fortunately, I often abandon my penchant for pragmatism to accommodate for my unwarranted superstitions. And since I only feel the need to act logically in selective situations, I am perfectly content with the illogical nature of my other habits:

Raised with my great-grandmother, grandparents, and parents all under one roof, I never lacked a consultant to help me transcribe Korean holiday dates from the lunar calendar onto my schedule. Yet whenever all four generations of my family celebrates with a traditional meal of *bulgogi*, my untraceable and admittedly nonexistent Italian blood flares in protest;

I rebelliously cook myself *linguine con le vongole* that clashes terribly with my mom's pungent *kimchi*.

If I plot a graph of "hours I spend in physical activity" versus "week of the year," the result looks like an irregular cardiac cycle. The upsurges symbolize my battles with colossal walls of water in hopes of catching a smooth surf back to Mission Bay shore. The ensuing period of rest mirrors the hours I spend researching in that one spot in my debate team's war room that isn't covered in papers (yet), or at the piano sight-reading the newest Adele song. Then the diastolic tranquility is interrupted by the weekends when I'm sprinting through trenches to avoid paint-balls swarming above my favorite arena at Paintball USA.

I find comfort in the familiar. I treasure the regular midnight chats with my brother as we indulge in batter while baking cup-cakes for a friend's birthday, keeping our voices hushed to avoid waking our mom and facing her "salmonella is in your near future" lecture. Yet, some of my fondest memories involve talking to people with whom I share nothing in common. Whether my conversations are about the Qatari coach's research on Kuwait's female voting patterns, or about the infinite differences between the "common app" and the Oxford interviewing process, or even about my friend's Swedish school's peculiar policy of mandating uniforms only on *Wednesdays,* I love comparing cultures with debaters from different countries.

My behavior is unpredictable. Yet it's predictably unpredictable. Sure, I'll never eat a Korean dinner like one might expect. But I'll always be cooking *linguine* the moment I catch a whiff of *kimchi*.

REVIEW

Despite suffering from a lack of cohesiveness, this essay is successful in breaking the typical boundaries of the college essay and giving us a sense of the individual behind the computer. The author starts off the piece using an exchange with a debate teammate about her clothes choice before a debate, which she uses as a starting point for a discussion of the "illogical nature of [her] other habits." The opening story is engaging because it rings with authenticity—it's a discreet way to indicate that debate means a lot to her.

The magic doesn't work as well with the other examples of illogical habits that the author brings up in the rest of the essay, however. What is illogical about liking to alternate surfing with debate preparation, for example, or liking to mix up the familiar with the unexpected? The anecdotes seem more like a way to draw attention to some of the author's achievements—surfing, piano—than an occasion to reflect on her "predictably unpredictable" behavior.

What saves the essay from sounding like a list of extracurriculars is the sizable dose of humor injected into the descriptions. The author's description of "the debate team's war room" and her "untraceable and admittedly nonexistent Italian blood" not only create vivid images in the mind of the reader, but also give off the impression she is poking fun at herself. Likewise, alternating mentions of such high and lofty topics as Kuwait's female voting patterns with descriptions of paintball and midnight baking sessions create the image of a young woman who has passions and goals, but who also knows not to take herself too seriously.

In spite of its choppiness, this essay thereby succeeds in a very difficult quest: making the author likable to the reader. It's a great illustration of the fact that writing a good essay should involve writing about things that mean a lot to you—whether it's dressing for debate tournaments, discussing Middle Eastern politics, or just baking cupcakes.

—Sarah Fellay

III. INTROSPECTION

These essays are characterized by the fact that they mostly take place inside the author's head. They're made up of thoughts and ideas and are often more abstract than other personal statements. A good introspective essay can hit on all the important goals of a personal statement while being unique and interesting.

Letting an admissions officer inside your head is a surefire way of keeping the essay focused on you. Good introspective essays help a reader get a sense for not just who you are as a person, but also how you think and what you think about. This can be either good or bad. For people with novel, impressive thoughts, it helps gain the admissions officer's respect. But at the age of seventeen, finding something to say that the admissions officer hasn't heard many times before can be difficult. Many essays of this variety run the risk of being overwritten. When big words and complicated metaphors are used ineffectively, an attempt to seem impressive falls flat. On occasion, this issue lessens the impact of the essays in this section.

Yet, introspection, when pointed and specific, can do exactly what is intended—give the reader a snapshot of a clear-thinking, interesting applicant with things to say and the ability to express them.

Rachael Smith

I am a scientist and I am an artist. I am a musician, an athlete, a philosopher, and an activist. I am a waitress and a world traveler, both a suburbanite and a citizen of the world. I fill so many roles and I have such varied interests that sometimes I am not sure who I am. Jack Kerouac describes these feelings best in his novel *On the Road* with the line, "All I have to offer anybody is my own confusion." The confusion of which Kerouac writes is an active confusion. He was not complacent in his uncertainty; he was a searcher. He traveled thousands of miles, seeking to understand the world and his place in it. He wrote of "offering" confusion, indicating a hope for reciprocity. Kerouac viewed his search as a collaborative process, looking for answers in the many diverse and interesting people he met along his journeys.

Like Kerouac, I am a searcher. This is a direct result of being raised in a Unitarian Universalist congregation. The Unitarian Universalist doctrine encourages uncertainty. Among other things, we affirm and promote the equality of all, persecution of none, and the free and independent search for truth. My upbringing instilled in me a sense of moral responsibility. It has taught me the meaning of service and the importance of respect. What has shaped me the most, though, is that idea of an "independent search for truth." Unitarian Universalism teaches that personal beliefs should be developed individually through consideration of diverse input, and that differences in beliefs should be not only respected but encouraged.

In my search I turn to everything for input: literature, music, films, world religions and politics, modern art, and almost every other form of pop culture imaginable. I have traveled to eight foreign countries, each expanding my global perspective. My most meaningful learning experiences, though, have been in interactions with other people. I am a very social and outgoing person. I tend to make friends with people from many different groups. I enjoy having many different friends because I am given the opportunity to see from diverse perspectives. For this reason I love meeting and getting to know new people.

This Kerouacian search for who I am and what I believe is something I hope to continue for the rest of my life. Already, it has made me a politically and socially aware person and instilled in me a passion for action. I hope to never stop learning, never lose my youthful curiosity, and never stop sharing in my confusion, because each new experience, new place, and new person I meet is a shared opportunity to learn. Perhaps by sharing in the confusion I will begin to find answers that work for me, or perhaps not. In the end, it is not the answers I'm interested in so much as enjoying the search.

REVIEW

Seeking inspiration in classic literature is a time-tested method for essay-writing. Rachael's multitudinous introductory interests would be overwhelming, but Rachael sums them up cleanly with a quote from Kerouac, explaining that the different directions she is being pulled in are confusing but also reassuring. This successful representation of her various interests and identities rarely comes through in a college application essay.

The way that Rachael connects her confused search for truth to her Unitarian Universalist faith is admirable—that part of the essay is genuine and well written. She is passionate about connecting to other people, about absorbing experiences so that she might be able to process the meaning for herself. She also uses the lessons she's learned from her religion to relate to her *On the Road* metaphor, supporting the relationship between herself and her lessons from both sources.

But in her comparisons to *On the Road*, Rachael's thesis loses direction. Perhaps her wandering and vague final paragraph is a result of the line that Rachael chooses to highlight from *On the Road:* "All I have to offer anybody is my own confusion," which is actually a misquote from the original Kerouac line, "I had nothing to offer anybody except my own confusion."

Rachael's conclusion is where she drives the essay home. By presenting herself as a searcher—in pursuit of knowledge and personal advancement—she succeeds in convincing a reader that she is the ideal member of a college community.

—Virginia Marshall

WINNIE WU

Soft Wooden Heart

The backbone of my life is my writing desk. I like to describe its surface as an organized mess (despite my parents' overdramatized description of a bomb site), a state of positive entropy and minimum energy. Math exercises overlap an organizer, set next to almost-empty tubes of paint and overdue library books. A constantly filled bottle of water sits behind a glasses' case full of guitar picks, and carved into a mountain of paper, right in the middle, is a space reserved for my laptop—on days when I am slouching, *The Complete Works of William Shakespeare* needs to be slid under it. An eclectic desk shows an eclectic personality; mine has had the honor of being the training grounds prior to the Great (final) Battle (exam) of Chemistry, the peaceful meadow of relaxed reading afternoons, and all in all the pristine-turned-colorful canvas of an inquisitive mind.

I remember buying it with my mother five years ago, when my bruised knees protested against the tiny white-paint-gone-yellow one I had used since childhood. My new desk was made of native Rimu heartwood—solid, resilient, dependable—a perfect role model for me to grow into. Over the years, its material became representative of my New Zealand identity, its surface slowly coated in quirky personality, and its compartments filled with treasured memories; the heartwood desk echoed my heart.

At first, it did not fit with the decor of the rest of my room, which even now appears boxy and stark next to my grandiosely elegant writing desk, but its quiet strength is unafraid of individuality, just as I have learned to become. It has watched as I grew stronger branches, a straighter trunk, firmer roots; whereas I had once been but a shy young

Introspection

seedling, I sprouted leaves and with them the ability and yearning to provide shade for others. I have certainly physically grown into it, but although I would like to think that I have become completely independent, I remain human; in inevitable times of need, it is still my steadfast, sturdy desk that offers its support.

I sit here and, well, I write: joyfully, desolately, irately, wistfully—at times paralyzed by excitement, at others crippled by fear. I scrawl notes in my organizer (which is, naturally, not in the least organized), words overflow my blog, overemotional oranges and blues plague my illustrations; shallow scratch marks indent the wood from where I have pressed too passionately into paper. It may be solid, but it is elastic enough to be shaped, resilient enough to adapt: This is my soft wooden heart.

It can take it. My desk remains constant despite scars of experience—unassuming, stoic, ever watchful. Even when I dismembered dying cell phones, their frail key tones pleading for mercy, the desk stood there, nonchalant. Regardless of what fervor goes on from time to time, it knows there will eventually be a constant calm; my lively nest of rebuilt mobiles still calls this place home. Sometimes, I rest my uncertain head on its reassuring solid surface and the wood presses back into my heartbeat, communicating in Morse: "Don't worry. Some things will never change."

And, like a mother, it always turns out to be right. Beneath my seemingly chaotic coat of papers and objects; beneath the superfluous, temporary things that define my present life, my desk and my heart remain still—solid, stable, and evergreen, ready to be written onto and scratched into by experience.

REVIEW

One of this essay's strengths is its honesty. Winnie manages to convey a lot about her life by describing what lies on her desk, from "empty tubes of paint" to guitar picks. She slips in important details about herself almost casually, letting us know that although she is studying for her chemistry exam, she also uses *The Complete Works of William Shakespeare* to prop up her laptop when she's slouching in her seat. Her skillful thick description makes her very real and quirky personality shine through: Winnie quips that her organizer is "naturally, not in the least organized," and she describes how she "dismembered dying cell phones" on her writing desk. Overall, Winnie does a successful job of conveying much about her character and personality through the description of a rather mundane and everyday object, her writing desk.

If this essay has a flaw, it is its lack of central focus or narrative structure. Winnie does attempt to tell a story over the course of her essay, using the writing desk as a motif to narrate the tale of her own development from a "shy young seedling" to a more mature young adult. Winnie's writing desk comes into her life as a "role model," remains in her room watching her mature and grow up, and serves as her metaphoric heart, remaining "solid, stable, and evergreen." Yet other than her hobbies, we learn little about what kind of experiences have shaped Winnie's "New Zealand identity," and her essay lacks narrative structure other than simply detailing Winnie's transition into maturity. Tracing a story line or centering the essay on a narrative with a beginning, middle, and end would help lend this piece the structure that it currently lacks.

Overall, however, Winnie successfully accomplishes the rather difficult task of setting the vibrant narrative of her own growing maturity on top of the description of an everyday and familiar object, her writing

Introspection

desk. Her essay paints a picture of her life that could stand to be more structured, but nonetheless conveys an interesting and multifaceted personality.

—Sandra Y. L. Korn

KEVIN DONG

Fields, farmlands, forests speed by. I catch glimpses of glimmering bodies of water. The beauty of it all stuns me and yearns for my exploration. Architecture passes by: expansive jetties, intricate bridges, quaint buildings. I wonder how these structures are built or even conceived of. Similarly, I ponder the existence of the complex machinery and myriad vehicles I spot from the train. Yet the overarching mystery that shrouds these sights is the unsung history behind each of them.

I pull myself back from the window, pleasantly overwhelmed by the spectacular view. Today I sit alone. I am journeying to my father's apartment, several states away. Shuttling between the companies of two loving parents, ironically without company. But I could not have asked for a better opportunity to meditate.

Opening my small notebook and with pencil in hand, I begin to explain my thoughts to the pages. I introduce the scientific law of conservation from which I derive my latest conjecture. The question: "If physical quantities such as energy are conserved, then is skill conserved?" The answer, I reason: "Yes." Every human being begins with the same net skill; when he or she excels in a particular activity, proficiency in another is lost to maintain balance. The apparent truth of this statement intrigues me as I consider its manifestations in society.

I suddenly begin to ponder its personal implications. Have I spread myself thin, like a dab of paint suffused across a broad surface? I like to dabble. I am so much more than just the academic on paper. I have checked on the ice, smashed a tennis ball, and raced in the waters. I play violin and sing in choir. I follow the news; I write creatively; I listen to music. I am an amateur video gamer and a budding tech geek, but also a grassroots environmentalist and a dedicated volunteer. And I devote what free time remains to my thoughts, my friends, and my family.

So much I have tried, so much I have learned, so much I have experienced. Yet I am neither an incompetent novice nor a world-renowned expert at any of these activities. I possess substantial skill in all and though I have not peaked, my interests have been piqued. I am just a high school student, sampling dishes and trying to figure out what he likes best.

I am just a high school student. My thoughts dissolve back into reality. In the vacant seat next to me, my backpack lies with my notebook tossed on top. In my hand, I contemplatively twirl my pencil. I look back out the window at the passing landscapes, now engulfed in twilight. I recall the racing thoughts from earlier today and realize that even in them, my interests were scattered. I am a curious puppy thrust into a beautiful new world. So what shall I do now? I will apply the next coat of paint and see where it dries thickest.

REVIEW

Kevin's essay is highly relatable—it is an endearing account of a person still very much undecided about the course of his life, a state that doubtless many college applicants find themselves in. Kevin has crafted a number of very beautiful sentences and images, and the flow of his writing is unique. Of particular note are Kevin's descriptions of what he sees outside of the train—his sentence, "Fields, farmlands, forests speed by," is elegant not only for its brevity, but for its mimetic similarity to how things are seen out of a fast-moving train. Still, at times the essay reads as though Kevin was trying too hard, with too many

SAT words and too little genuine feeling behind them. Sentences like, "I introduce the scientific law of conservation from which I derive my latest conjecture," attempt to prove that Kevin is intelligent, and the essay loses its relatability in the mire of unnatural language. Kevin's writing is at its best when it's clean and simple; where he strays from this, the prose can become overwrought, and distracts from Kevin's message.

Furthermore, some of the clarity of Kevin's essay is lost in too many metaphors. For example in his last paragraph, Kevin describes himself as a puppy, and then two sentences later resolves to "apply the next coat of paint" as if he were an artist? Even without the mixed metaphors, his last sentence might be difficult to understand for a harried admissions officer—his last reference to the paint metaphor appeared a number of paragraphs earlier. Kevin's image of "paint suffused across a broad surface" is a novel and interesting one—had he pruned away his many other comparisons and instead concentrated and developed this one, his essay would have made gains in both style and clarity. Kevin's essay thus serves as a good lesson in both its successes and its failings: In a medium as short as a personal statement, natural-feeling language and a clear, unified vision are key.

—Erica X. Eisen

CARRIE TIAN

The best compliment I ever received was from my little brother: "My science teacher's unbelievably good at telling stories," he announced. "Nearly as good as you." I thought about that, how I savor a good story the way some people savor last-minute touchdowns.

I learned in biology that I'm composed of 7×10^{27} atoms, but that number didn't mean anything to me until I read Bill Bryson's *A Short History of Nearly Everything*. One sentence stayed with me for weeks: "Every atom you possess has almost certainly passed through several stars and been part of millions of organisms on its way to becoming you." It estimates that each human has about 2 billion atoms of Shakespeare hanging around inside—quite a comfort, as I try to write this essay. I thought about every one of my atoms, wondering where they had been and what miracles they had witnessed.

My physical body is a string of atoms, but what of my inner self, my soul, my essence? I've come to the realization that my life has been a string as well, a string of stories. Every one of us is made of star stuff, forged through fires, and emerging as nicked as the surface of the moon. It frustrated me no end that I couldn't sit down with all the people I met, interrogating them about their lives, identifying every last story that made them who they are.

I remember how magical it was the first time I read a fiction book: *Harry Potter and the Sorcerer's Stone*. I was duly impressed with Quidditch and the Invisibility Cloak, of course, but I was absolutely spellbound by how much I could learn about Harry. The kippers he had for breakfast, the supplies he bought for Potions—the details everyone skimmed over were remarkable to me. Fiction was a revelation. Here, at last, was a window into another person's string of stories!

Over the years, I've thought long and hard about that immortal question: What superpower would you choose? I considered the usual suspects—invisibility, superhuman strength, flying—but threw them out immediately. My superhero alter ego would be Story Girl. She wouldn't run marathons, but she could walk for miles and miles in other people's shoes. She'd know that all it takes for empathy and understanding is the right story.

Imagine my astonishment when I discovered Radiolab on NPR. Here was my imaginary superpower, embodied in real life! I had been struggling with AP Biology, seeing it as a class full of complicated processes and alien vocabulary. That changed radically when I listened, enthralled, as Radiolab traced the effects of dopamine on love and gambling. This was science, sure, but it was science as I'd never heard it before. It contained conflict and emotion and a narrative; it made me anxious to learn more. It wasn't that I was obtuse for biology; I just hadn't found the stories in it before.

I'm convinced that you can learn anything in the form of a story. The layperson often writes off concepts—entropy, the Maginot Line, anapestic meter—as too foreign to comprehend. But with the right framing, the world suddenly becomes an open book, enticing and ripe for exploration. I want to become a writer to find those stories, much like Jad Abumrad and Robert Krulwich from Radiolab, making intimidating subjects become familiar and inviting for everyone. I want to become Story Girl.

REVIEW

Carrie begins her essay with a classic paradigm that is often successful in college admissions essays. She suggests that she is different, quickly noting that her unique penchant for stories is inherently absent in others. It's a solid essay for sure, incorporating her interest in science with a very specific anecdote about her high school biology class that brings an especially personal touch to her writing. She breaks the fourth wall as well, using the phrase "as I try to write this essay"— a risky, but effective statement, in this case. Colloquialisms are strung throughout the piece; contractions are commonplace, establishing a casual feel that adds to the conversational nature of the piece. These gambles work for Carrie, as they make her a likable and relatable narrator, which is not always the case when a student speaks directly to the reader.

However, the transition between thoughts is one of the weaknesses of her essay, and it shows when she quickly switches between descriptions of atoms, Harry Potter, and superpowers. Granted, these ideas are connected by the overarching theme of "stories," but nevertheless, moving between each is jarring. She gives the reader just a moment to consider flying around on a broomstick before bringing up the concept of a variety of other superpowers that she has dreamed of over the years. It is then that she describes her desired superpower as the ability to tell stories, and ties this together with her interest in science and academics. Yet, there is little preparation for any of these ideas, and while it again seems conversational and friendly to keep bringing in these new points of fascination, the structure somewhat detracts from the essay.

Another risk that she takes is pointing out a potential academic weakness late in the essay. In order to demonstrate her status as a storyteller, she chooses to share that she initially found AP Biology to be a struggle due to its content and the obscurity of some of the vocabulary involved in the course. This is not necessarily an issue here, since she qualifies her statement by explaining that viewing academics through the lens of a story allows her to understand concepts that initially would seem foreign. However, doing this incorrectly could easily lead an admissions officer to develop a negative impression of the applicant. As it is written in this case, the statement suggests that Carrie can not only creatively come up with methods to master material, but she also can be effective at communicating with others throughout her studies, summing up an essay that expresses an impressive individual's passions and interests.

Her willingness to present her flaws alongside her strengths gives the impression that Carrie is presenting herself fully. The positives she writes about herself are more believable as a result of this. The strategy works awfully well, and gives the essay a fitting conclusion.

—David W. Kaufman

Danielle Lessard

Why a Republican Read The Communist Manifesto

I am a conservative. Point-blank. I'm not talking "hardcore, no gay marriage, abortion equates to eternity in Hell, Catholicism is the only religion worthy of my acknowledgment" conservative, but I believe in limited government intervention in private business. I may seem like an unlikely candidate for such beliefs; I live in Springfield, Massachusetts, an urban environment where the majority of the population utilizes some sort of government assistance to supplement the costs of living. Well, maybe not the absolute *majority*, but I certainly see a lot of it. Though raised as a Catholic, I believe in nothing more than simple spirituality, and do not abide by all the stipulations of the strict Catholic community (although I do continue to attend church because I find the environment welcoming and the people overwhelmingly happy and uplifting). I attend the Drama Studio, a small, conservatory style acting community where I am considered the token Republican (artsy *and* conservative—is this what Harold Camping meant by the Rapture?) Not surprisingly, my colleagues have made many attempts at conversion ("Watch MSNBC, Danielle; I promise you'll love it!") But I stick to my guns—no pun intended. However, I have found that sharing the majority of my time with those of conflicting opinions has enlightened me in the ways of respect and compromise.

Enter Jacob Mueller. Literally the son of a preacher man (his father is the minister at Trinity United Methodist Church), his political views on Facebook are listed as "Member of the Communist Party of America." Oh, boy . . . He entered my Advanced Scene Work class in its second semester, and as is the Drama Studio custom, I welcomed him with open arms and commenced what I soon discovered to be the long and interesting process of getting to know him. Through this, I discovered a few important things; like me, he loved politics. Like me, he was well informed. And, like me, he was more than willing to argue his opinion.

Through our *Odd Couple* dynamic, we found an endless number of conversation topics. Every day was a new, "Did you see what the Tea Party's newest legislation entails?" countered by a, "How about that Scott Brown, eh?" I was the Michele Bachmann to his Al Gore. But the remarkable thing about our debates was not their intensity or their depth, but how much I was *learning* by listening to him talk.

A strange thing was happening to me. For the girl who had always been staunchly opinionated and stubborn, who had never been one for agreeing with the opposition, who took pride in her ability to stand her ground even when she represented the minority view, compromise suddenly had a new meaning. Its connotation was no longer negative. And, in turn my ability to not only understand but also respect a view contradictory to my own was growing in strength.

In order to foster this newfound mind-set, I presented myself with the ultimate challenge. In a moment of excited passion, I logged on to Amazon.com and, for $4.95, ordered a copy of *The Communist Manifesto*. The little book, with its floppy laminated cover depicting a hammer and a sickle on a glossy black background and plain white block letters spelling out its title with inconspicuous innocence, took its place at the head of my bed, where it resided for the next month. Bit by bit, it began to fill with marks of pensive notation, speckles of yellow appearing in odd places where the highlighter had bled through, its fragile pages curving with the insistent pen marks that filled their margins.

As I devoured the words of Marx and Engels, I realized something remarkable. I'm not going to tell you I agreed with them; in a lot of instances, I didn't. But I *did* understand what they were saying, and

I was able to respect them both as visionaries *and* intellectuals. Where the old voice in my head would have said, "Wow, what idiots," my new voice was open to more than just the fundamental ideas, but the intelligence it must have taken to form them and the thought process behind them.

When I register to vote, I will not be registering as a Democrat. You won't see me at any PETA meetings, and you certainly won't hear me speaking fondly about President Obama's plans for health care. But I can proudly say that *The Communist Manifesto* taught this Republican what it means to compromise, and to respect.

REVIEW

This essay does a marvelous job of describing the way in which one's outlook on life can change over time. She takes thoughts about her evolving conservative political beliefs and turns them into something interesting by introducing other characters and using humor throughout.

Danielle's asides are funny in all the right ways. They generally poke fun at her conservatism without being offensive. Her line about being both artsy and conservative is a good example of using humor to convey aspects of one's personality that may not be immediately apparent in an essay. She's a not-too-conservative person who's also fairly witty? Check.

Her humor also makes the essay exponentially more enjoyable to read. Serious diatribes about changing ideals are fine, but descriptions that are actually entertaining are far more memorable.

It should be noted that though the essay is about Danielle and her ideological refinement, her use of other people (namely, Jacob) in her narrative makes the story seem far more credible, and makes her seem more relatable. Her interactions with Jacob showcase her ability to compromise and carry on successful interpersonal relations in spite of glaring political differences.

The essay would have benefited from more development at the end. Her interaction with *The Communist Manifesto* would have been slightly richer had we glimpsed a little more insight into her thoughts rather than her just saying that she disagreed with most of it. Was there a part that she found redeeming? While a relatively small critique, more elaboration would ensure that readers would not be left hanging at the conclusion in an otherwise excellent essay.

—Charlotte D. Smith

ALYSSA CHAN

I sit on a low, black bench, shifting and rustling about—settling in. Eighty-eight black-and-white keys stretch before me, filling the whole of my gaze. I look up to see my face reflected and distorted in the shiny, over-glossed black surface of the piano. I shift my eyes to the white pages in front of me, with their thin, dark, horizontal lines. Notes sit on these lines complacently in a manner that seems incongruous with their fluttering lightness when played. I raise my hands, fingers poised, and I am startled by the profoundness of this moment, knowing that at any instant I can press my fingers down on these keys and produce something from nothing; beauty from emptiness. It is often said that to be able to create music is one of the greatest joys in life. I agree; there is little I have experienced that can compare to the swell of notes forming rolling waves of melody, the current sweeping raw emotions out into the open and transforming them, making beautiful everything along the way. But, to me, this joy is and will always be second to something greater: the glory of that moment before a single note is played, when I sit before the piano, fingers outstretched in anticipation.

There are so many of these moments in life, small and unassuming, but all-consuming at the same time; little pieces of our parents telling us anything is possible, slivers of dreams in which we can do anything. We often look past this *moment before*, diving right into the action; we marvel at the splendor of a concert, overlooking the startling beauty and harmony of an orchestra tuning; we are so transfixed by the sunrise that we forget about the incredible promise of the dull morning gray. But it is in these instants of anticipation, the *moments before*, that we unexpectedly glimpse what is possible without the interference of fear or reality. I know that the dreams of these moments do not always come true; many hopeful beginnings end with disappointment and failure. I know also that as I grow up, experience may persuade me to not believe in fairy-tale endings. But I hope that I retain some of my idealism, if only in these small fragments. I strive to carry a sense of optimism forward with me, holding onto the momentary feelings of radiant innocence that allow me to believe in endless possibilities.

My seventeen years have been spent preparing for now; the melody of the rest of my life is about to begin. I hope that one day I'll look back on this time and reflect on the anticipation, the brilliance that had yet to emerge. As I sit here writing this, I realize that *this* is the *moment before* . . . and I can't wait.

REVIEW

Alyssa's essay is unique in both its content and in its delivery. Rather than focusing on an "unusual experience" (a ubiquitous topic in college essays), she instead examines a relatively ordinary one—at least for personal statements—from a creative and unexpected angle. Her exquisitely detailed description and beautiful turns of phrase transcend the everyday and add depth to what could easily have been an extremely uninteresting narrative. But it is not her eloquence alone that distinguishes this essay—it is her decision to emphasize the "moment before" rather than the moment itself. What initially seems like a nicely worded take on an overdone topic becomes an unexpected and refreshing look at how moments are experienced.

Despite its overall excellence, Alyssa's essay could benefit from a couple of revisions. Some of its sentences, particularly toward the end of her second paragraph, border on the cliché; structuring the essay in such a way that they were more spread out might have lessened the effect. The metaphor she draws from the anticipation she describes to her life more broadly feels rushed; it may have been better to shorten the initial description in order to develop her main point more fully. As it is they feel a bit disconnected since the transition is so abrupt and the final paragraph so short, but she does manage to include some words (particularly the allusion to music) that tie the essay together nicely.

However, Alyssa does an excellent job in creating an essay that illustrates her personality through both its style and its substance. The primary strengths of this essay lie in its eloquence. Although many essays become pretentious in their quest for poeticism, Alyssa combines lovely phrases with an overarching simplicity that prevents her writing from growing too flowery or otherwise overpowering. Her second paragraph, in which she explores in greater detail her always-italicized *"moment before,"* is not preachy or pompous. Her elegant prose always maintains readability.

On the whole, Alyssa does an excellent job in creating an essay that illustrates her personality through both its style and its substance.

—Christina M. Teodorescu

JUSTINE LIU

When I was a child, I begged my parents for my very own Brother PT-1400 P-Touch Handheld Label Maker to fulfill all of my labeling needs. Other kids had Nintendos and would spend their free time with Mario and Luigi. While they pummeled their video game controllers furiously, the pads of their thumbs dancing across their joysticks, I would type out labels on my industrial-standard P-Touch with just as much zeal. I labeled everything imaginable, dividing hundreds of pens into Ziploc bags by color, then rubber-banding them by point size. The finishing touch, of course, was always a glossy, three-eighths-inch-wide tag, freshly churned out from my handheld labeler and decisively pasted upon the numerous plastic bags I had successfully compiled.

Labeling became therapeutic for me; organizing my surroundings into specific groups to be labeled provides me with a sense of stability. I may not physically need the shiny color-coded label verifying the contents of a plastic bag as BLUE HIGHLIGHTERS—FAT, to identify them as such, but seeing these classifications so plainly allows me to appreciate the reliability of my categorizations. There are no exceptions when I label the top ledge of my bookshelf as containing works from ACHEBE, CHINUA TO CONRAD, JOSEPH. Each book is either filtered into that category or placed definitively into another one. Yet, such consistency only exists in these inanimate objects.

Thus, the break in my role as a labeler comes when I interact with people. Their lives are too complicated, their personalities too intricate for me to resolutely summarize in a few words or even with the 26.2 feet of laminated adhesive tape compatible with my label maker. I have learned that a thin line exists between labeling and just being judgmental when evaluating individuals. I can hardly superficially characterize others as simply as I do my material possessions because people refuse to be so cleanly separated and compartmentalized. My sister Joyce jokes freely and talks with me for hours about everything from the disturbing popularity of vampires in pop culture to cubic watermelons, yet those who don't know her well usually think of her as timid and introverted. My mother is sometimes my biggest supporter, spouting words of encouragement and, at other instances, my most unrelenting critic. The overlap becomes too indistinct, the contradictions too apparent, even as I attempt to classify those people in the world whom I know best.

Neither would I want others to be predictable enough for me to label. The real joy in human interaction lies in the excitement of the unknown. Overturning expectations can be necessary to preserving the vitality of relationships. If I were never surprised by the behaviors of those around me, my biggest source of entertainment would vanish. For all my love of order when it comes to my room, I don't want myself, or the people with whom I interact, to fit squarely into any one category. I meticulously follow directions to the millimeter in the chemistry lab but measure ingredients by pinches and dashes in the comfort of my kitchen. I'm a self-proclaimed grammar Nazi, but I'll admit e. e. cummings's irreverence does appeal. I'll chart my television show schedule on Excel, but I would never dream of confronting my chores with as much organization. I even call myself a labeler, but not when it comes to people. As Walt Whitman might put it, "Do I contradict myself? / Very well, then I contradict myself, / (I am large, I contain multitudes.)."

I therefore refrain from the temptation to label—despite it being an act that makes me feel so fulfilled when applied to physical objects—when real people are the subjects. The consequences of premature labeling are too great, the risk of inaccuracy too high because, most of the time, not even the hundreds of alphanumeric digits and symbols available for entry on my P-Touch can effectively describe who an individual really is.

REVIEW

The first thing that jumps out about this essay is the topic. While other college applicants might offer their profound thoughts on life, love, and the human condition, Justine begins with a slightly less sexy topic: labeling stuff. She readily admits that it's a bit of an eccentric hobby; as she says in her essay, label makers are to her what video game consoles are to much of the rest of the teenage demographic. The unorthodoxy of it, though, is precisely what makes it so captivating. The essay draws the reader in with a topic that, at a very minimum, is intriguing. This immediately puts Justine, the writer, in the incredibly advantageous position of having a story that people actually want to read.

Complementing her distinctive choice of topic, Justine has an infectiously quirky style that truly shines through in her writing. Her vocabulary is sprinkled with little idiosyncrasies, making it easy to imagine her as a child as she "decisively pasted" labels onto "successfully compiled" bags, proudly basking in her triumphant success. Justine's use of specific, geeky details is quite endearing, a kind of lightheartedness that makes a reader laugh just a little bit inside while following along. As she describes her Brother PT-1400 P-Touch Handheld Label Maker, the 26.2 feet of label-maker tape, or her bag of "Blue Highlighters—Fat," readers get a powerful sense of her youthful enthusiasm for labeling.

Her subsequent shift from labeling as hobby to labeling as stereotyping—while an attempt to provide some additional substance to the essay—is less memorable. While her anecdotes about her labeling hobby are original and refreshing, her discussion of labeling people feels a bit trite. She essentially observes that labeling people is wrong because people are not one-dimensional, a well-worn platitude. It was a safe choice. But was it the best?

Instead, Justine could have improved her essay by focusing on what makes her stand out, namely her creative, quirky personality. After all, a successful college essay needs not to draw any deep philosophical conclusions about the world—its main purpose is simply to bring the writer's unique voice to life. Nevertheless, Justine does a terrific job expressing herself as an individual, infusing her essay and her application as a whole with a warm and distinct personality.

—Victor C. Wu

JOHN FINNEGAN

Why I Went to the Rain

Drops hurtled from the sky, splattering the window with futile attacks as I gazed out at the dusk. I looked up at the clouds, trying to gauge how long and how hard the rain would fall, wondering whether the thunder and lightning would rumble on or settle in. Satisfied that they would linger, I stepped out into the evening, my feet resting upon the cold steps of my soaked stairway. As raindrops pelted my head and saturated my shirt, I watched a torn and trembling sky. It was a nice view.

Standing in the rain, I was separated from the rest of the world. Peering up at drops of water, I thought only of those drops, only of how they cooled my face and quieted my mind. The storm, in all its might and force, swept away the rest of the world. The squall left me in darkness, but not in a cold, unfeeling, dreadful night. The shadows of a storm are inherently alive, filled with energy and existence, molecules and matter. While destruction could follow behind, it had no place in the storm itself, no place in the vitality that surrounded me. In my storm, I was not thinking of downed power lines or flooded basements—those thoughts were pushed aside, overcome by the noise and rain. As thunder boomed in the heavens, I left behind thoughts of the future and concerns for my livelihood; all I knew was the beauty and joy of life.

That night, I found serenity in chaos. I lived. The storm forced me to be concerned solely with the present and revel in that concern. In the storm, I discovered freedom, but the freedom I chanced upon was that of simplicity, not irresponsibility. For once, I knew what I wanted: to stand quietly a little longer as the storm thundered on.

While I neither tap-danced nor sung in the rain that night, I stood, walked, and enjoyed the water running from my forehead to nose, streaming down my face into a mouth longing for cool liquid. In a world where most of my life is spent indoors, separated from anything wild or uncontained or free, the storm presented an opening of the cage that contains my spirit.

Yet, the tempest comes rarely, and when it comes it stays for minutes, not hours. Until the rain returns, I wait indoors and enter a world filled with demands both complicated and exhausting. There, I scurry about, trying to juggle the competing commands of my parents and friends, school and society. The requests for attention mount up, piling into hills that I chisel slowly away, turning from one to the next, struggling to keep up with the twists and turns of the maze I call life. But, locked away in the subconscious mind of John Finnegan, a desire remains. It does not fade, no matter how long the dry spell or how hot the summer. It remains, and it longs for storms.

REVIEW

John ventures to provide a glimpse into the complex psyche of the exhausted student. He takes a risk as he grapples with such a universal phenomenon, at least among the demographic of students that apply to these institutions. He risks committing the two major sins of the college essay: perpetuating a cliché and seeming disingenuous. The admissions officer can't help but ask: How realistic is it that a high school student experiences such a perfect moment of reflection, complete with overarching symbolic parallels?

Already at a disadvantage, he dares to continue down a risky path. There is thunder, lightning, and a "torn and trembling sky." There is reflection on the destruction of a tempest and personification of its parts. There is even a juxtaposition of serenity and chaos, freedom and concerns. At any moment, I expect the heroine from the latest romance movie to dramatically run into John's embrace, as he twirls her in the pouring rain.

Interestingly enough, however, it is in these risks that the author finds his greatest strengths. He ultimately avoids both issues by consciously tackling the overdone; as he says, he neither "tap-danced nor sung in the rain that night" but rather stood. Then, he meticulously interjects with those aspects of himself that make him most vulnerable: his fears. He brings the very personal into the personal statement. We learn little about his accomplishments or qualifications, and he is wise to avoid the laundry list. Yet, we walk away with a profound understanding of who he is at his core. In doing so, John produces a work that demonstrates his command of prose while maintaining the integrity of his message.

—Fatima Mirza

IV. OVERCOMING OBSTACLES

Stories about overcoming obstacles are common among personal statements, and there's a reason for that. When done well, these essays can be the best of the best. They give admissions officers a chance to get to know you as a person—really the ultimate goal of the personal statement—and give you a chance to demonstrate how impressive you are. The struggles students generally explore in these essays may not have been revealed to admissions officers in any other context, and for that reason, essays on overcoming obstacles add to applicants' credentials without running the risk of bragging.

The thing to watch out for: If you're going to write about overcoming obstacles, you better have something good. In this section, you will see one student's essay on fibromyalgia—a chronic syndrome without a cure that causes widespread pain across the body—next to an essay about a student's struggle with anemia—in this case, a disease easily treated with a daily iron supplement. Comparatively, the student with anemia seems to have overcome very little.

The best of these essays, though, don't just make the student sound impressive for what he or she has accomplished under trying circumstances. The best essays do all of this, while also weaving in the parts of that student's personality that are not defined by either the obstacles or the successes. Sometimes, this is done by incorporating a little humor into even a very serious essay. Sometimes, it is done by including the applicant's hopes for the future as well as his or her struggles in the past.

The essay on overcoming obstacles is not appropriate for everyone, but the great ones will stand out.

LAZARUS D.

I used to have a commemorative coin set for 1994, the year I was born. Silver dollar and half dollar, quarter, dime, nickel, and penny, all sparkled inside the protection of a clear Lucite case. It must have been given to me when I was very young because I cannot recollect any of the details of receiving the gift. What I can remember is how shiny those coins were in 2001, when we cracked the case open so that we would have food to eat over a long weekend. I will never forget the tears my mother shed as she cried, "Sorry. I am so sorry," over and over again. The $1.91 in change bought ten packs of Top Ramen and a box of frozen vegetables—food I was grateful for.

My mother should have been a doctor. But, right out of high school, she married my father, a man significantly older than her, believing he would provide her with freedom and the financial support so she could pursue medical school. In reality, she had married a man with no job and no ambition, who was a drug addict and alcoholic with a violent temper. As a little boy, I would watch him go into rages and break everything he could get his hands on. His diet consisted of Jack Daniel's, cigarettes, M&M'S, and any pill he managed to get a hold of. My mother left him when I was five and my sister was two. I have rarely seen him since.

To say that life has been a struggle would be an understatement. My mother, sister, and I have been homeless on several occasions. With all of our belongings packed in the back of the car, we have bounced from house to house with friends and friends-of-friends, sleeping on the living room floor, in a spare bedroom, or a tent in the back-yard. We have also had periods of more prosperous times where my mother could afford an apartment and gas service, but not power. A few years ago, we spent six months using battery-operated lanterns, rarely staying up after the sun went down. This left me little free time, and it made completing my homework an immediate priority.

In all of this, I have held close the mantra that my mother has repeated to me throughout my life, "The two most important things in life are your education and integrity. Once they are yours, they can never be taken away." My sister and I have always been told that school is the top priority in our lives. Even with family and household upheaval, we have stayed in our neighborhood schools. My mother has made countless sacrifices to keep that portion of our lives steady. I realize the struggles she has faced on our behalf and in return, have strived to take full advantage of the free education provided to me.

It's not always easy finding the time to study. My mother often works three to five jobs at a time, so I am responsible for taking care of my sister, who has a heart condition. I have to help her maintain her diet, exercise routine, and medications, or else she is at high risk for having heart attacks.

My major educational goal has been to attend a top university as a math and physics double major. My area of interest is specifically in laser technology and how improvements can be made to help with major surgeries, such as cardiac and neurosurgeries. I want to create advances in lasers that will not only save lives, but also improve the quality of life for millions. I want be able to study the most cutting-edge science with the brightest minds in the world. And ultimately, when I reach my goals and create new laser technology, it will save my sister's life.

REVIEW

In choosing to write a highly personal essay, Lazarus ensured that his statement would not mimic any other personal statement submitted to Harvard. His life struggles relate extremely important things about who he is as a person and student. The opening description of the Lucite case of coins readies the reader for a story about a hobby or a childhood toy. The story then makes a surprising shift in tone and focuses on extreme hardship as the coins become symbols of Lazarus's loss of innocence. He quickly becomes an adult and saves childish things for his father—the man who only eats M&M'S.

Lazarus's willingness to open up about such a difficult time in his life is admirable and certainly creates a personal narrative that holds up the essay and informs the reader. The first two paragraphs paint a dark picture of a life and what is surely an important aspect of who Lazarus is as a person—which is, of course, the key element of a personal statement. The final paragraphs of the essay turn into a description his sister's illness and his desire to help surgeons. Important things to be sure but perhaps too much to tag onto the end of an essay that already carries so much.

Conversely, his quick mention of academics works extremely well. For many Harvard essays, any time spent defending the importance of academics would seem out of place or redundant. Lazarus's quick mention of such a thing, however, could be vital. Hardships overcome do not appear on an academic transcript—this essay not only informs who Lazarus is as a person but also allows the admissions officers to see his entire application with a new understanding.

—Amy Friedman

HANNAH UMANSKI-CASTRO

I am sitting on the end of a cafeteria table. My company is a familiar face: a new library book. At the table behind me, my classmates are laughing. When I attempt to join them, they all fall silent, avoiding my questioning glance. Tears well up in my eyes. "Why is this happening to me?"

This was a common scenario throughout my grade school experience, though it climaxed in fifth grade, in a small class of only seventeen kids. The fifth grade was the year everyone was obsessed with conformity. I never did fancy Follow the Leader. Maybe it was because I lived in an apartment complex, and did not own clothes from Abercrombie & Fitch. Maybe it was because I was the bespeckled girl whose nose was constantly lodged in a book. I loved school, and I loved reading; thus, I became an easy target.

Sometimes, I wondered why they bullied me, why they purposely excluded me from their conversations and their company, when they did not even know me. Now, I understand that they acted the way they did *because* they did not know me. They did not comprehend how much I valued my education. They did not know that because the post office was losing business, my dad was working fewer hours, and that every penny he made he stretched to pay for our food, the bills, and my school's tuition. They did not know that my mom could not work because she was taking care of my baby sister and my aging grandmother. Above all, they did not know what an education meant to my mom, who left her home country of Costa Rica before she graduated from college so that she could earn enough money to support her parents.

"*Cariña*," my mom would say, "an education is the most important gift your father and I can give you. We make sacrifices so that you and your brother and sister can have a better life, and make a better future for yourselves. With an education, you can be whoever you want to be. You can achieve your dreams!" It was a philosophy etched in my heart.

How could I best fulfill my dream? Despite being labeled an outcast by my classmates, I decided to take the initiative. I reached out and became an active participant in my school community. By taking advantage of the opportunities my school had to offer, I discovered my strengths and passions. In addition, I developed a keen sense of fairness, and an ability to identify and reach out to others who are feeling left out. These experiences helped me grow into a confident young woman, unafraid to stand up for what I believe in, ready to do whatever it takes to fulfill my dreams. Wherever I go in the future, I shall strive to listen and learn from all my experiences, without forgetting who I am.

REVIEW

The five-hundred-word limit is Hannah's greatest foe. Her aim: to communicate a tale of bullying, to explain the extra-bullying hardships she had to face, and to weave it all together to produce an optimistic, press-on-regardless mind-set. It's a feat to do *one* of those effectively in five hundred words, and this multitasking tale is strong and focused in spite of that barrier.

The present-tense opening establishes her alienated suffering. It *is* hard for her to ascertain exactly what she should be conforming to other than a disdain of education, and she concludes that it is her peers' ignorance of her home life that preempts the bullying. As a study in form, the introductory veneer of a knowledge-loving young girl behind a library book pitying her bullies for their uncompassionate ways shows that the crux of the essay is not this love of education—a seemingly perfect desire for admission into Harvard—but the even more empathic love for fellow human beings, most notably her family. And though Hannah does not have enough space to communicate years of struggle, the crafting of her sentences lends the piece some urgent candor.

The end of the essay does have a rushed, vague feel. We don't know what passions she has developed and how she reached out and "became an active participant." However, this seems more to be the effect of a writer who thought what she wrote before was too negative, and thus the positive recompense must be illustrated in Technicolor. For the young woman who had an uneasy high school career and internally created pressure to succeed for her family, she traces the ravine and the ascent for the reader to follow. Her empathic capacities to make others identify with her plight are on display, just as she claims she strives to do.

—Christine A. Hurd

Sarah Chapin

I am standing behind my high school when a snowball pelts my side with a thud and splatters across my jacket, covering me with a fine, icy dust. My bewildered eyes trace the snowball's trajectory until they fall upon a pair of snickering hoodlums crouched behind a small mountain of snowballs. They must have been waiting all afternoon for an unsuspecting student to walk by, and perhaps for emphasis, one of the boys looks me in the eye and raises a grimy middle finger. Quickly, I mold a handful of snow into a sphere with cupped hands and cock my arm back.

I haven't thrown anything in a while, but muscle memory guides me through the requisite motions. I played softball for eight years, and my athletic strength was always my throwing arm; in fifth grade, when my coach asked me to throw the ball from third to first, I hurled the ball with such force that the catch knocked him off-balance. Upon entering high school, it seemed natural that I would play on the school's softball team.

However, my body had other ideas. Throughout middle school I'd developed increasingly painful body aches, and in freshman year I awoke one morning with a brutal headache penetrating the crown of my head and the bones of my face as though a vice had been clamped to my skull overnight. After consulting more doctors than I can remember, I was diagnosed with fibromyalgia.

Fibromyalgia is characterized by chronic widespread pain and extreme sensitivity to touch. My neurologist describes fibromyalgia as "headache of the body." Personally, I favor my father's description;

after one particularly painful and exhausting day he aptly proclaimed, "Fibromyalgia is your body's way of giving you the finger."

Agonizing muscle cramps mocked me constantly, preventing me from walking longer than five minutes without growing exhausted. The pressure above my eyes sneered at me whenever I attempted to read or write. Even after I found medications to temper the headaches just enough so I could return to school with sporadic attendance, sharp pains gnawed at my body with haughty derision if I even thought about returning to the softball fields and the activities I loved.

For months I tried to ignore the cruel obscenities fibromyalgia hurled my way, steadfastly believing the pain would soon subside and I would achieve everything I had planned for myself if I simply disregarded the taunting aches and worked doggedly to catch up at school. But when softball season arrived, it became apparent that while determination and intelligence could preserve my GPA in the face of fibromyalgia, there was no personal attribute or skill that could heal my body and allow me to join my teammates on the field.

It was time to confront the beast.

In doing so, I kept in mind the schoolyard aphorism that there is strength in numbers. I did not face fibromyalgia alone, but with mathematics by my side. Baseball is a game of statistics, and if fibromyalgia threatened to steal the sport I loved through physical deterioration, I would outsmart this insolent illness and reclaim ownership of baseball through intellectual pursuits. I began a mathematical research project, analyzing the effectiveness of current baseball statistics, as well as deriving my own.

Fibromyalgia forced me to redefine my goals and personal standards for success. This baseball project was my first step toward reclaiming my life and laying the foundation for victory over my illness. As calculations replaced pitching drills, my passion for baseball was channeled into a burgeoning love of science and math. Hours I had previously devoted to softball became filled with scientific journals and books, and summers I used to spend at athletic camps were devoted to research at local universities. Baseball provided a link to my pre-fibromyalgia life at a time when I desperately needed one, and through baseball I realized that if I wanted to beat fibromyalgia, I could not simply hope it would disappear overnight. Whether I modified my medications or adapted my schedule, I needed to devise my own way to face fibromyalgia's antagonizing aches head-on.

So when that taunting rascal waves his middle finger in my direction, my cheeks do not flush with angry humiliation and my legs do not run away, but my hands mold a snowball and my arm pulls back. As I follow through with my throw, pain radiating up my arm, I know instantly that I will pay for this exertion in the morning. But my icy comeback hits the sniggering boy squarely in the chest, knocking him backward into the snow as his accomplice's mouth lies agape in shock.

Well. I guess I've still got it.

REVIEW

Sarah's story opens with a vivid anecdote of being pelted by a snowball that brings the reader to the scene of the crime with detailed sensory descriptions. She skillfully ties the story to her talent for athletics, which in turn leads to her struggle with fibromyalgia and how in the face of physical limitation she redirected her passions to science and math. The story comes full circle and ties together nicely at the end with the conclusion of the snowball scene, which leaves the reader feeling victorious and vindicated for Sarah, as well as proud of her determination.

Sarah manages to cover a lot in this essay. The personal statement is an evident combination of overcoming obstacles and discovering academic passions, and also discreetly includes résumé-worthy accomplishments, such as her own mathematical research project on baseball statistics and summer research at local universities. What is important about her personal statement is that she goes beyond the résumé and gives the admissions officers a look at her character and personal struggle.

Even though her essay is a bit long, Sarah does not waste a word and ensures that every detail she includes contributes in some way to the overall message she is trying to convey about herself.

Rather than simply evoking sympathy for her situation, Sarah weaves humor and a cheeky attitude throughout her narrative. She introduces her love of mathematics with a creative twist on the common saying, "strength in numbers," and affectionately alludes to her father's depiction of fibromyalgia as "your body's way of giving you the finger."

Her vivacious and tenacious personality shines through in her colorful and descriptive language, painting a clear picture of Sarah as a determined person who doesn't let a chronic illness defeat her and instead finds another passion.

—C. C. Gong

DAVID ROBERTS

"Let's face it, you're slow," my violin teacher said.

He was, as always, complaining that running was detracting from my practice time.

That summed up what running had always meant to me, ever since I was a seventh grader, choosing his sport for the first time. I was fine and content, however. I always had Jeffrey and Archie, classmates like me who ran slowly. We were good friends. We laughed together; we raced together; we pushed each other, and endured tough workouts together. But after middle school the people I trained with went on to do things they were better at. I remained, even though I was not good enough to be considered for varsity.

High school running was hell. I struggled with workouts, most of which I had to run alone. In the hot, dry days of autumn, I often coughed on the dust trails left by my teammates as they vanished into the distance. During the workouts, I got passed incessantly, almost getting run over on occasion. It hurt not to be important; to be dead weight for the team. I looked forward to the next year, when I could hopefully run with the incoming freshmen.

It didn't happen that way. Even a year later, I was *still* the slowest on the team. How could the freshmen who had snored off the whole summer beat me, a veteran from middle school and high school with decent summer training? I nevertheless reconsidered the effectiveness of my training, and looked forward to getting "back in shape." It was only after my condition had been deteriorating steadily for a few weeks that I began to feel a new level of humiliation. I started to have trouble keeping up with old ladies in the park, and each day I worked frantically to prevent the discovery of that fact by my teammates, running toward the sketchy areas of the ramble, in the south, where there's barely anybody. My mother, worried about the steady deterioration of my condition, contacted a doctor.

I was anemic.

The doctor prescribed a daily iron pill, and the results were exhilarating. I joked that I was taking steroids. I sunk into endless oxygen. I got tired less. During the workouts, I felt more machine than man. Iron therapy taught me something fundamental. It reminded me why I was running; why I had stuck to this damn sport for four straight years. When I was anemic, I struggled to gather what little motivation I had for those painfully slow jogs in those parks. Putting the effort in, and seeing the dramatic results fooled my mind like a well-administered placebo. Iron therapy was the training wheels that would jump-start my dramatic improvement.

It took four months—four months of iron pills, blood tests, and training—to get back to my personal best: the 5:46 mile that I had run the year before.

Early February that year, the training wheels came off. I was running close to seven miles a day on my own. But I wasn't counting. I could catch a light. I could walk as many stairs as I wanted without getting tired. I was even far ahead of where I was the year before. After two and a half years as a 5:50 miler, I finally had a breakthrough race. I ran a 5:30. I asked coach if I could eventually break 5 minutes. He told me to focus more on maintaining my fitness through spring break.

I ran the mile again, this time outdoors. Coach had me seeded at a 5:30. I ran the first lap, holding back. I didn't want to overextend myself. I hoped to squeeze by with a 5:35. The euphoria was unprecedented as I realized by the second lap that I was a dozen seconds ahead and still holding back. I finished with a 5:14.

On the bus ride back from the meet, one of my long-standing dreams came true. I pretended to ignore Coach sitting next to me, but he kept on giving me glances. He was excited about my time. We talked a lot about the race. We talked about my continuous and dramatic improvement. He said it was early in the season and that I would break 5 minutes after only a few weeks of training.

Six weeks later, Mr. Song, my chemistry teacher, asked me if I had broken 5 minutes for the mile yet. I told him all about how I had run in three meets over the past month and had failed to break 5:15 on every one of them. I told him that 5 minutes was now for me a mirage in the distance. Mr. Song, however, did not show much concern: "You're just overtrained. Once you ease up before the big meet, you'll drop in time once more."

Even though these consoling words were from the man who had baffled my nutritionist when he had guessed that I was anemic, I still doubted his wisdom. On Sunday, I would run the mile once. My last mile of the year. This was it. Using my tried-and-true racing strategy, I finished with a 5:02, a 12-second drop in time. Mr. Song's predictions had again turned out to be correct.

Before I was anemic, the correlation between hard work and success was something that only appeared in the cliché success stories of the talented few. Now, I am running more mileage than I ever have before. And my violin teacher still complains.

But I smile. I know it's going somewhere.

REVIEW

David's opening sentence of "'Let's face it, you're slow,'" blends welcome humility with an assumed question. This mystery propels the first half of the essay: namely, "Why is David slow?" It's an admirable strategy from the start, as college admissions essays usually approximate a brazen "Hardship X and/or Triumph Y Made Me an Übermensch." Yes, this essay is of those stripes as well, yet it tempers what could be an egotistical display with an attractive dose of self-deprecation. For example, in the first sentence, the assumption is not that slowness is the hardship; rather, it is that he has to face the fact that he is trying too hard and should probably stop doing as such. But we all like someone who has so much earnestness, they must be told to quit.

The first half of the essay exhibits mastery over creating reader interest and flows from thought to thought with ease. We have a mystery, a struggle, and a familiar tone that does not smack of presumption. David's climactic reveal of the cause of his slow-running speed is a surprise—handled with mature self-awareness that an iron deficiency isn't the same as cancer or loss of limb.

Ironically, once David's physical capacity is restored in the essay, the essay becomes anemic itself. Who is Mr. Song? If Coach's approval was so important, why was he not mentioned pre-diagnosis? Too many elements are thrown in as auxiliary support to David's victory lap. This leads to an odd contrast to his plain message of hard work equaling success. For where were all of these people when he was working hard but *not* succeeding? Before the diagnosis, it was his friends and his mother; why are these other authority figures coming out of the woodwork in the eleventh hour? Moreover, the quantification of success—only obsessed with numbers and times—takes the heart and soul out of his prose.

Though David starts off strong, his final lap leaves a reader wishing he had stopped halfway through, and is a fair warning to applicants to make sure to stop when they are ahead.

—Christine A. Hurd

Eda Kaceli

Homeless for Thirteen Years

I sat on my parents' bed weeping with my head resting on my knees. "Why did you have to do that to me? Why did you have to show me the house and then take it away from me?" Hopelessly, I found myself praying to God realizing it was my last resort.

For years, my family and I found ourselves moving from country to country in hopes of a better future. Factors, such as war and lack of academic opportunities, led my parents to pack their bags and embark on a new journey for our family around the world. Our arduous journey first began in Kuçovë, Albania, then Athens, Greece, and then eventually, Boston, Massachusetts. Throughout those years, although my family always had a roof over our heads, I never had a place I could call "home."

That night that I prayed to God, my mind raced back to the night I was clicking the delete button on my e-mails, but suddenly stopped when I came upon a listing of the house. It was September 22, 2007— eight years exactly to the day that my family and I had moved to the United States. Instantly, I knew that it was fate that was bringing this house to me. I remembered visiting that yellow house the next day with my parents and falling in love with it. However, I also remembered the heartbreaking phone call I received later on that week saying that the owners had chosen another family's offer.

A week after I had prayed to God, I had given up any hopes of my family buying the house. One day after school, I unlocked the door to our one-bedroom apartment and walked over to the telephone only to see it flashing a red light. I clicked PLAY and unexpectedly heard the voice of our real estate agent. "Eda!" she said joyfully. "The deal fell through with the other family—the house is yours! Call me back immediately to get started on the papers." For a moment, I stood agape and kept replaying the words in my head. Was this *really* happening to me? Was my dream of owning a home finally coming true?

Over the month of November, I spent my days going to school and immediately rushing home to make phone calls. Although my parents were not fluent enough in English to communicate with the bank and real estate agent, I knew that I was not going to allow this obstacle to hinder my dream of helping to purchase a home for my family. Thus, unlike a typical thirteen-year-old girl's conversations, my phone calls did not involve the mention of makeup, shoes, or boys. Instead, my conversations were composed of terms, such as "fixed-rate mortgages," "preapprovals," and "down payments." Nevertheless, I was determined to help purchase this home after thirteen years of feeling embarrassed from living in a one-bedroom apartment. No longer was I going to experience feelings of humiliation from not being able to host sleepovers with my friends or from not being able to gossip with girls in school about who had the prettiest room color.

I had been homeless for the first thirteen years of my life. Although I will never be able to fully repay my parents for all of their sacrifices, the least I could do was to help find them a home that they could call their own—and that year, I did. To me, a home means more than the general conception of "four walls and a roof." A home is a place filled with memories and laughter from my family. No matter where my future may lead me, I know that if at times I feel alone, I will always have a yellow home with my family inside waiting for me.

REVIEW

Eda's essay captures the reader's interest immediately with the startling title, "Homeless for Thirteen Years." It intentionally sets misleading expectations; she is not homeless in the traditional sense of lacking a roof over her head, but in the sense of not having a true house to call home. Her readers become emotionally invested in the story, worried for the fate of the girl weeping and desperately praying on her parents' bed. Eda soon reveals that though her family has suffered hardships, she has not spent her life living on the streets. This disparity draws attention to her point that a home is more than "'four walls and a roof,'" but at the cost of potentially downplaying the situations of those who are traditionally "homeless." The technique serves her well enough, but beware of rhetorical devices that may be unintentionally misconstrued.

Additionally, Eda's essay at times delves into cliché. It would be improved with more nuance about her definition of a home, lest it begin to sound like a dictionary entry. Avoiding phrases like "No matter where my future may lead me" or "not going to allow this obstacle to hinder" would further strengthen the prose.

However, Eda's essay consistently engages her readers. Her theme is compelling by its own right; the idea that home should be "a place filled with memories and laughter" is easily appreciated. But she doesn't present this theme as an abstract ideal. Rather, she concretely describes her desires to host sleepovers and to have a room to gossip about, and her longing to have a familiar place where her family will always be waiting inside. Eda's essay grabs its readers and keeps them emotionally invested. It makes them care.

—Indrani G. Das

ARAN KHANNA

A Cut Below

Standing at a whopping five and a half feet high, I am not very tall. Now this might not sound like a glaring, life-changing confession, but to the rowing community this fact can make or break everything. I don't fit the mold of a traditional rower. In fact, at first glance there is nothing that separates me from being a coxswain. I am short, extremely light, not particularly burly, and loud (a must in a good coxswain). So when I meet fellow oarsmen and tell them I am a rower it is no wonder that they usually scoff at me. So why do I do it? Why do I decide to put myself at a disadvantage and row? The answer is that I really *want* to have an oar in my hands. So I push myself and my teammates in every workout and race. I am constantly fighting people taller and stronger than me to be the better rower. To me rowing has nothing to do with innate skill. There is a simple correlation between teamwork, hard work, and success, and nothing can supersede that. Through my hard work and the support of my teammates I now realize how much I have accomplished. I worked my way into the light eight that went to Youth Nationals, and I, the smallest rower on the team, was elected to represent it as captain. Looking back, I realize that rowing has taught me the value of perseverance and teamwork, and those are things that I have readily been applying to almost every facet of my life.

The perseverance I have learned from rowing has allowed me to tackle many issues that I previously would have given up on, from fighting through the frustration of trying to teach English in a Chinese village to doggedly attacking a difficult math problem. This sense of determination has allowed me to view failure as a step toward success rather than something to fear. Perseverance has become an integral part of who I am and how I face problems.

As a rower I know that a well-performing team can achieve much more than any individual, and this idea constantly affects me as I go throughout my day. Running the school newspaper, leading Lakeside squash club, and even working on homework, are all activities that I approach as a teammate, rather than as an individual, because of rowing. Just as I constantly try to unify any boat I am rowing in, I feel that I am always pushing friends and classmates to work together. This notion of teamwork and collaborating with others is one that has led me to become an effective leader and conquer many challenges.

The struggles I have faced while rowing have profoundly influenced me and taught me some of the most valuable lessons of my life. The skills I have learned from rowing have influenced the way I approach problems and will be a part of me for as long as I live.

REVIEW

Aran's essay takes the shape of an onion. It begins with an outer coating that draws the reader in and proceeds with a series of substantial inner layers—each of which reveals deeper insight into Aran's character.

The physical description of Aran serves as the perfect external layer, because it depicts him as the athlete who is at a major disadvantage because of his size; the rower who is looked down upon by other rowers, the oarsman who is constantly mistaken for a coxswain—as the underdog—(*everyone* loves a good underdog story). Once the essay effectively engages the reader this way, it seamlessly transitions into the narrative's second and third layers: Aran's analysis of his athletic experience through the lens of his struggle as the unlikely rower and the contextualization of other aspects of his life—such as teaching, squash, and journalism—with respect to perseverance and teamwork, the two values he learned to appreciate through rowing. The strength of his essay rests with this structure; by creating a burgeoning self-portrait of Aran, the onion-like organization style of the narrative enables Aran to impart to the reader a detailed and comprehensive understanding of who he is by the end of the essay.

The only risk Aran takes is not taking any risks at all. After reading countless essays that predictably expound upon students' résumés by demonstrating their abilities to rise above challenges and collaborate efficiently with their peers, admissions officers likely welcome bold attempts at the new and unusual. Aran's essay, written in a simple, straightforward, and even somewhat conversational tone, lacks such an audacious venture. This essay contains no fanfare, no theatrics, no drama—but it does get the job done.

—Maddie Sewani

Scott Lazarus

I will be elected to the office of President of the United States of America.

I'm more than qualified—in fact, I've been groomed for the position my entire life. I know this because God and the California court system have provided me with a fertile training ground—time spent under the stewardship of a half-absentee father and a psychopath of a grandmother.

In fact, it was my father's absenteeism, which provided me with my first lesson in presidential effectiveness. Every Sunday, he gave me the opportunity to practice my patience (a skill undoubtedly necessary in dealing with Congress) as I waited at the door for his arrival. I resorted to television as a means of passing the time, watching PBS telethons as a substitute for cartoons. I often mirrored the volunteers on the screen, calling number after number, trying desperately to reach my father. But as voice mails and dial tones subsided to the agonizing silence of loneliness, I succumbed to failure.

On the rare occasion that my dad remembered my existence, I would be taken to his place of residence: my grandmother's home. It was there that I attended weekly tapings of *The Jerry Springer Show* and learned how to wage war. Arguments began with the topic of a loan, and would often, if I was lucky, end with a visit from the police. My father was India, my grandmother Pakistan, and "Stupid b****!" a nuclear assault. To my family, Mutually Assured Destruction came in the form of mutual restraining orders.

Often, I even got the opportunity to hone my diplomatic skills. Being asked to choose a side was a special treat (though a difficult decision, as neither side offered an oil incentive), and supporting one faction meant treason to the other. Being disowned by my grandmother was a regular occurrence, as was someone leaving in tears. I can still feel them on my face. However, pain was of no consequence—I believed these lessons to be worthwhile and necessary.

But these "lessons" are not what have pushed me toward Washington. I've gained a much greater gift from my family's dysfunction.

I must assure you that the first line of this essay was not one of aspiration. Nor was it written for the purpose of shock. Rather, it is a statement of fact. A statement used both as a tool to find meaning in my childhood and to express the only thing in my life that I know to be an absolute truth.

Ingrained within me is the need to transcend mediocrity. To give to humanity, rather than take. If I've learned anything significant from my Sunday/Wednesday family, it's that I want to do more with my life than collect a monthly welfare check. Quite selfishly, I want to reach the Oval Office to dispel my own fears of failure. However, the true source of my motivation lies in a deeper need to create positive change. To know that, when all is said and done, I have left the world a better place. I won't settle for anything less.

REVIEW

In his essay, Scott successfully combines a tough childhood experience with a blunt statement of his professional ambitions. Although the personal background–lesson formula is so popular that essays in this genre run the risk to become repetitive and boring, Scott keeps the reader engaged by recounting sad childhood moments using a well-crafted political lexicon. This makes the description of painful situations like the absence of his father and the family disputes fresh and original, while drawing an unexpected parallel between those and the presidential office. Because the merits of praiseworthy family members are a recurrent motif in personal statements, Scott's focus on his family's "dysfunction" instead makes his entrance essay stand out.

The daring and pretentious-sounding opening statement is tempered by the clever use of ironic expressions throughout the first part of the essay, as in the "PBS telethons" and the "weekly tapings of *The Jerry Springer Show*." While revealing the author's resilient personality, the irony does not diminish the gravity of Scott's experience. The "agonizing" silence and the tears underscore the pain the applicant has endured, as does the conclusion of the essay, where Scott admits that his conviction to become president reflects the need to rise above the "mediocrity" that his family represents. Those who scoff at the very first line of the essay will change their mind by the concluding paragraphs, where Scott's genuineness and maturity shine.

—Francesca Annicchiarico

V. FOREIGN LIFE

The most commonly clichéd essay topic—traveling to another culture—is such a common story line that it is almost worth avoiding. Particularly cliché are the essays about traveling to do good for the less fortunate. The story line is so played out that in order to impress an admissions officer with your accomplishments, you would probably have to cure poverty or a life-threatening disease. But since digging a well or framing a house—noble as it is—appeared in so many of the essays that were submitted to us for selection, we felt the need to pick apart what worked and what didn't so you can plan your course of action most effectively. While it will be difficult to wow admissions officers with this course, you can impress them by describing the effect of the experience on you.

Being a foreigner can also make for an interesting and original essay. In this section, some applicants will explore what it means to be different, some will explain how good-hearted others can be, and one delivers a refreshingly light account of her time in France.

If you can avoid the overdone and find something new to say, writing about experiences abroad or as an outsider allows you to present yourself as a strong, brave person who is not afraid to try something new.

SF

Three Bundles of Affection

Humans share a universal craving for proteins wrapped in carbohydrates. Each culture creates its unique form, from samosa to sushi to ravioli, to satisfy this yen. My story involves three types: dumpling, *bistek kalabaw* burger, and *cuajada empanada*.

I cherish memories of my childhood in Beijing involving my extended family making the ubiquitous dumpling together. Eating was secondary to the simply magical process of dumpling manufacturing. Water, flour, and stuffing would be minced, kneaded, flattened, and folded, morsel by morsel, into perfectly flavored bites. Each person was roped into the assembly line. Amid the chatter of Mandarin gossip, the grumbling of the rolling pin over dough, and the melodious simmering of water, I, the mere six-year-old, proudly stood on my stool as the indispensable doughball-maker, beaming at my relatives while my little hands frantically rolled the pieces of dough into perfect spheres.

After immigrating to the United States, my small family of three struggled to multitask all these steps, while nostalgically reminiscing about our life in China. But the new dumpling-making unit soon absorbed friends of all races as adopted aunts and uncles, sisters, and brothers. After a period of laughing over clumsy mistakes and misshapen products, the assembly line works as flawlessly as the original. I know that I will always carry with me the dumpling tradition wherever I go as an everlasting tribute to my heritage.

Life in America has allowed me ample chance to enjoy hamburgers. Yet my favorite burger-eating experience occurred thousands of miles away in the Philippines. Its ingredients included an eclectic mix of pandesal bread, carabao meat (*bistek kalabaw* in Tagalog), and cucumber slices, an unintentional culinary tour de force made from the only ingredients available in the village of Dugui Too. There, enclaved deep in the mountains of Catanduanes, people make a bare subsistence, living with no semblance of a modern infrastructure. On the trek in, we waded through rivers where women were immersed waist-deep washing clothes. Throngs of noisy kids followed us, admiring our lighter skin and hair. Our distribution of solar lights there met with a primitive fascination. In a few hours, we were able to mingle with the timid but warmhearted locals despite the language barrier. Seeing their faces alight in excitement for the solar lights filled my heart with wondrous joy. The *bistek kalabaw* burger represents the delirious happiness at the rare privilege to be able to touch people's lives so palpably.

It was halftime into my six-week immersion program in Nicaragua when I came down with a severe fever. I was temporarily forced to abandon my humanitarian duties and rest uselessly in the isolated village, where literacy, technology, and medical care were nonexistent. I closed my eyes to tolerate the pangs of my headache amid a torrential downpour. On a sudden whisper, I reopened them wearily. With surreal clarity, I saw a plate of dumpling-like morsels, dreamlike after twenty days of monotonous tortillas and beans. My host mom pointed with her lips in the typical Nicaraguan manner with such sweet words: "*Son empanadas, pruebelas.*" I ventured a bite, relishing the unfamiliar corn shell filled with Nicaraguan sweetened *cuajada* cheese. Only by thinking back did I realize the generosity of these indigent people. My host brother had trekked three hours on the sinuous mountain trail amid the thunderstorm, just to bring back the ingredients, which cost more than the daily wages of the entire family. They must have carefully planned the surprise, putting together all the money to take care of a complete stranger. The selfless love infused into these empanadas cemented my connection to the Nicaraguan family that adopted me as its own.

The dumpling, the *bistek kalabaw* burger, and the *cuajada empanada*, ordinary food as they are, matter so much to me. Each symbolizes a bundle of care and affection from a culture I consider my home.

REVIEW

In SF's essay, we're guided through three stories, each neatly corresponding to a carbohydrate-wrapped protein. SF's words are beautifully evocative, transporting us into the kitchens of Beijing, through the mountains of the Philippines, and to the villages of Nicaragua. Each story exposes part of SF's personality: The dumplings show she cherishes her heritage and cultural roots. The burgers showcase her selflessness and compassion for those less fortunate. The empanadas reveal she recognizes and appreciates the generosity of others.

SF is a gifted writer, but her descriptions are occasionally guilty of excessive romanticizing. Phrases like "wondrous joy," "delirious happiness," and "selfless love," even when accurate, can seem like they're trying a bit too hard.

This is also a long essay, weighing in at 655 words. Her decision to exceed the word count limit is understandable, considering she chose to synthesize three detailed stories, but risky. She teeters dangerously close to a topic that is too ambitious. Her stories feel truncated, each leaving fundamental questions unanswered. Why is she distributing solar lights in the Philippine village of Dugui Too? What is her immersion program in Nicaragua? The transitions are quite abrupt because of the limited space, and her theme of carbohydrate-wrapped proteins isn't referenced in her conclusion. A hundred more words could have tied up these loose ends, but would blatantly violate the word count rule. Be careful when scoping your topic; it works in this case, but barely.

Her conclusion, though terse and rushed, recognizes the power of her stories, and resists the common urge to draw unnecessary connections. She doesn't need to list off her desirable characteristics and accomplishments for her admissions officers. SF gives her stories space to speak for themselves. We're left with a very real, very positive sense of who this person is.

—Nikhil L. Benesch

DANIELLE FEFFER

Teammates

I wrap my scarf more firmly around my neck, feeling the chill of the brisk January air as I trudge my way to practice. The bus stop isn't actually that far from the pool, but with a heavy backpack and the fancy shoes that my host sister insisted I wear, the three-minute trek seems to last forever. Turning the corner three blocks down, I finally make it to the parking lot and see one of my friends.

"*Salut,* Thomas."

He knows that it's me without even looking. "*Salut,* Danielle." He finishes fiddling with his bicycle lock and stands to greet me. I lean in for my customary kiss, and he obliges, *bisous*-ing me once on each cheek, before we walk toward Piscine Bréquigny together.

Easy conversation flows between us as our well-trained feet follow the paths to our respective changing rooms. I punch in the code on the girls' side and open the door. Familiar figures stand in various states of undress, and *bisous* go all around while we change and speculate on the various tortures Marc will put us through today. Then we head down to the pool deck, ready to meet our fates.

I get to our coach first, and mentally switch back into English. "Hey, Marc, what's up?"

He shrugs. "Fine."

I laugh and give him a high five, then move on to *bisous* and *ça va?* the rest of the boys. When I get to Islem, who is Algerian, the two of us proceed to execute our exceedingly complex non-French secret handshake, recently perfected at Tours during last week's three-day meet. (We foreigners have to stick together, after all.) We end with a perfect fist bump, and I smirk.

Islem winks back at me. *"Et ouais."* That's how we roll.

Marc eventually yells at us to get to work, and we all start to put on our caps and goggles. I pull out my team cap from home, reflecting on how much I've changed since I left. Four months ago, I was mute, standing awkwardly to the side, hoping that English instructions for the new and frightening social interaction would suddenly appear out of thin air. Now, flawless French rolls off my lips as I greet my friends, laughing freely at inside jokes, not thinking twice about kissing swimsuit-clad swimmers on the cheek. I'm not just *on* the team anymore—I'm *part* of it, and every single *bisous* reminds of that fact.

Someone pushes me into the pool and my shriek is swallowed by the water. I surface and swear my revenge, glaring all the while at Pierre, the obvious culprit, who is grinning unabashedly. Then he yelps and falls as he himself is pushed in as well. The whole team eventually follows us into the water to start the day's warm up, and a small smile, fond and content, flits across my face before I join them.

REVIEW

There is one sentence in Danielle's essay in the past tense: a brief reflection on her stunted French four months prior to the scene described. The breezy dismissal of those worries in the rest of the essay has a certain *je ne sais quoi*, admittedly; however it makes for a strange personal statement. Persuasive essays as a form are often easier to grasp and consider when they are declarative ("Pick me because of this.") or contemplative ("Let us think about this lobster and convince you to pick me because of my prescient observations about said shellfish."). This is neither. There is no reflection as to how she felt before her experience in France; there is sparse description of her interiority in general.

Foreign Life

But this refusal to engage with the standard mechanisms of personal statements makes Danielle's essay stand out. It seems alternatively attractive because of its refusal to conform to a seemingly prescribed formula and disappointing because of its reliance on long chunks of hapless dialogue in order to create an interesting plot.

The essay's strength is its tone: Danielle writes just casually enough to allow a reader to enjoy the essay, and creates a refreshing read, maybe because of, rather than in spite of, its lack of angle. But it is a risky move, and one that could backfire. The safer path, for Danielle, would have been to write about something more concrete. Her willingness to try something different worked for Danielle and produced a high-quality essay.

—Christine A. Hurd

JOSH PALAY

I look over at the digital clock at the front of the bus just as the time changes to 8:30. The engine begins to rumble, the seat begins to shake, and the bus slowly pulls onto Route 6 and heads toward JPA—the Jay Pritzker Academy—near Siem Reap, Cambodia. The bus is alive with chatter. Peace Corps volunteers trade stories about their experiences in their assigned villages; international schoolteachers discuss their plans for the day's lessons. I overhear one of the Peace Corps volunteers, Deidre, say, "I have to say, the Peace Corps offers incredible health care. They medevaced me to Bangkok when I got dengue fever."

Today, I find myself unable to join the conversation. I stare blankly at the blue cloth seat in front of me, trying to gently coax my knotted stomach out of my throat. All I can think about is the empty seat beside me and the uncomfortable feeling of entering uncertain territory alone.

My friend and co-teacher, Shahriyar, is in the Angkor Hospital recovering from a serious bout of amoebic dysentery. I visited him yesterday. He was lying in bed with his summer reading in his right hand and an IV in his left. Looking pale and exhausted, he weakly lifted his head and greeted me. "I don't know if you know this yet," he said, "but I'm flying home tomorrow. Are you coming with me?" Though the news didn't surprise me, the question caught me off guard. As I left the hospital room, I couldn't help but think how easily this could have been me in his situation.

The bus drives over a speed bump faster than it should have, and I'm jolted back to the present. I try to take my mind off Shahriyar and look out the window at the world around me. Everything is so much different than it is in Deerfield, yet it all somehow feels very natural to me. To my left I see an elderly woman wearing a mask sweeping dust off the street; I smile at her, but she doesn't notice. As the bus gets closer and closer to JPA, the fact that I will have to teach today's lessons by myself begins to set in. I wonder if I'm physically capable of teaching three hours of class by myself in the ninety-degree heat and 90 percent humidity. In the past, Shahriyar and I had always taken turns leading the class, giving each other a few moments to rest and rehydrate while the other taught. A part of me is afraid to do it. I've never had to lead the class without the comfort and support of having Shahriyar by my side. As I think about the challenges I will face, I realize how easy it would be to turn back. I only have to call Sokun—a local *tuk-tuk* driver—and he'd take me to the airport. Knowing my co-teacher has become seriously ill, nobody would think less of me if I went home today.

As I sit in my seat, planning my trip home, the bus slows nearly to a stop and then turns onto a narrow red dirt road. I've suddenly plunged into a new world. The mess of worn-down concrete buildings and mopeds gives way to miles of flooded rice paddies stretching as far as I can see. Every few hundred yards I see boys and young men working barefoot in the fields. The bamboo huts that dot the landscape make me think back to my visit to the house of one of my students, Dari. I remember looking into his room and seeing a wooden table on his dirt floor. Close by, a bamboo shelf was filled with books. The globe he had won for being on the Honor Roll was proudly displayed on the bookshelf among his prized possessions. Smiling ear to ear, he told us that JPA was the best thing in his life. I realize that it really is too late to go home. I've already fallen in love with my students.

As the bus pulls into JPA's driveway, the rest of the teachers begin gathering their materials. I remain seated, deep in thought. "Are you coming?" I hear a familiar voice ask me. I look up and see Deidre looking at me.

"Of course I am."

REVIEW

In essays about community service, it is easy to fall into the trap of self-aggrandizement—emphasizing your own personal sacrifices and good deeds and in the process making yourself look like someone more interested in self-service than community service. Josh's essay, on the other hand, steers well clear of this pitfall, skillfully conveying compassion, humility, and devotion to the people with and for whom he works—he does not stay on because he pities his students, but because he loves them. As a result, instead of coming off like résumé padding, Josh's work feels motivated by a genuine desire to do good.

Structurally, Josh's essay is solid—it traces the trajectory of his thought process from uncertainty to renewed resolve. This seemingly straightforward story arc is enlivened by choice details and images—the off-hand conversation about dengue fever in the first paragraph, for example, adds a good jolt of surprise, and the descriptions of the Cambodian countryside are vivid and well-executed. The passage detailing Josh's visit to his student Dari's home is one of the essay's highlights, a scene that is both believable as the essay's "inspiration moment" and memorable for the deep empathy it contains.

While it's true that Josh has the advantage of a rather unique experience—not every Harvard applicant is in a position to write their personal statement about volunteering with the Peace Corps—the main strengths of his essay are certainly translatable beyond this context. Josh's essay is a personal statement at its best: it not just narrates an experience but hints at deeper elements of his personality and expresses them in a way that does not come off as forced. Someone reading Josh's essay can tell that his volunteering experience was far more to him than résumé fodder. And as the admissions office gets deluged with more and more applications every year, this spark of sincerity goes very far indeed.

—Erica X. Eisen

Lucien Chorde

I sat under the table, burying my head tightly in my folded arms, while the other children sat on the carpet, listening to the teacher's story. The language barrier was like a tsunami, gurgling with strange and indistinguishable vocalizations. Elementary school wasn't as fun as I expected at all.

"Hello?"

Hearing a whisper, I raised my head up, only to notice a boy's face merely inches away. I bolted up in surprise, my head colliding gracefully with the underside of the table. Yelping in pain, I noticed that the entire class was staring at me.

That was the story of how I met my first friend in Canada.

That boy, Jack, came to visit me during my lonely recesses. It was rather awkward at first—I could only stare at him as he rambled on in English. But it was comforting to have some company.

From there, our friendship blossomed. Our initial conversations must have been hilarious to the hapless bystander. Jack would speak in fluent English while I spurted sentence after sentence of Mandarin. It was like watching tennis—rallies of English and Mandarin back and forth. But I learned quickly, and in no time I was fluent.

Jack also showed me the ropes of Western culture. Heaven knows how embarrassing my birthday party would've been if he hadn't told me about those so-called "loot-bags" beforehand.

Today, I volunteer at a community service agency for new immigrants where I work with children. I do it because I understand the confusion and frustration of dealing with a strange and sometimes hostile environment; I remember how it feels to be tangled up in an amalgam of unfamiliar words and sounds. And so I teach them; I give seminars on reading, writing, and speaking skills as well as Western culture, history, and sometimes, a bit of social studies.

But I strive to do more than just that. I try to be a friend—because I remember how Jack helped me. I organize field trips to the science center, the museum, and the symphony: double-whammy trips where children can have fun while improving their literacy skills.

Through these experiences, I try to understand each of them as unique individuals—their likes, dislikes, pet peeves, background.

Everyone needs a guiding light through the lonesome process of adaptation, a friendly bump to lift them from the dark shroud of isolation. That's what Jack did for me—with a rather painful bump to the head—and it's also what I do for these immigrant children.

My hope is that, one day, these children will also feel compelled to do the same, helping others adapt to an unfamiliar environment. With this, we can truly create a caring and cohesive network of support for the children of our society.

REVIEW

Lucien's essay depicts a personal connection with his community service activity and provides the why to an extracurricular that probably shows up as only one line on the activities portion of his college application. He starts off with an endearing anecdote of meeting his first friend in Canada and connects the encounter to his current passion, then delves even deeper by concluding with self-reflection and a bigger goal for society that he hopes to achieve. His personal statement gives the reader a glimpse at his background and assimilation into a new culture, and how his own experience as an immigrant motivates him to help other immigrants adapt to life in a new place.

The strengths of this essay lie in the vivid and charming recounting of his first encounter with Jack, his first friend in a foreign new environment, and how he uses that story to explain his passion for volunteering. He connects his community service to a bigger goal at the end of the essay that leaves the reader feeling inspired, and alludes to his thoughts, hopes, and dreams. There is a tone of humility and humor as he depicts how he met his first friend by bumping his head under the table, and makes a motif out of the head bump by referring to it again later when he's talking about helping other immigrant children. He modestly credits his noble deeds at the community service agency to meeting his first friend, and humbly reveals his hope that his own good deeds will inspire others to pay it forward. He does a good job of exhibiting his accomplishments in community service without sounding like he's bragging.

Lucien could also make the essay more memorable and distinctive by including anecdotes of his experiences at the community service agency where he gave seminars and organized field trips. He denotes his volunteering responsibilities in list form, which can seem a bit impersonal and résumé-like. For example, he mentions how he tried to understand the people he helped, but does not include how he goes about doing this, or whether learning about those unique individuals contributed to his experience. Adding a story of how he changed the lives of the immigrants he helped would enhance his message and create a fitting parallel with the anecdote of how Jack helped him as he assimilated into Western culture.

Overall, Lucien combines humor with humility and leaves the reader feeling inspired.

—C. C. Gong

ALEX FOOTE

Look Through Closed Doors

I entered the surprisingly cool car. Since when is Beijing Line 13 air-conditioned? I'll take it. At four o'clock in the afternoon only about twenty people were in the subway car. "At least it's not crowded," one might have thought. *Wrong.* The pressure of their eyes on me filled the car and smothered me. "看看！她是外国人！" (Look, look! She's a foreigner!) An old man very loudly whispered to a child curled up in his lap. "Foreigner," he called me. I hate that word, "foreigner." It only explains my exterior. If only they could look inside. . . .

They would know that I actually speak Chinese—not just speak, but love. They would know that this love was born from my first love of Latin—the language that fostered my admiration of all languages. Latin lives in the words we speak around the world today. And translating this ancient language is like watching a play and performing in it at the same time. Each word is an adventure, and on the journey through Virgil's *Aeneid* I found that I am more like Aeneas than any living, dead, or fictional hero I know. We share the intrinsic value of loyalty to friends, family, and society. We stand true to our own word, and we uphold others to theirs. Like Aeneas's trek to find a new settlement for his collapsed Troy, with similar perseverance I, too, wander the seas for my own place in the world. Language has helped me do that.

If these subway passengers understood me, they would know that the very reason I sat beside them was because of Latin. Even before Aeneas and his tale, I met Caecilius and Grumio, characters in my first Latin textbook. In translations I learned grammar alongside Rome's rich history. I realized how learning another language could expose me to other worlds and other people—something that has always excited me. I also realized that if I wanted to know more about the world and the people in it, I would have to learn a spoken language. Spanish, despite the seven years of study prior to Latin, did not stick with me. And the throatiness of French was not appealing. But Chinese, more than these other traditional languages, intrigued me. The doors to new worlds it could open seemed endless. Thus I chose Chinese.

If these subway passengers looked inside me, they would find that my knowledge of both Latin and Chinese makes me feel whole. It feels like the world of the past is flowing through me alongside the world of the future. Thanks to Latin, Chinese sticks in my mind like the Velcro on the little boy's shoes in front of me. If this little boy and his family and friends could look inside, they would understand that Latin laid the foundation for my lifelong commitment to languages. Without words, thoughts and actions would be lost in the space between our ears. To them, I am a foreigner, "外国人" literally translated as "out-of-country person." I feel, however, more like an *advena*, the Latin word for "foreigner," translated as "(one who) comes to (this place)." I came to this place, and I came to this country to stay. Unfortunately, they will not know this until I speak. Then once I speak, the doors will open.

REVIEW

Alex has taken a freeze-frame of a moment on a train in China, and harnessed it as an opportunity to talk about her love of languages. It's a clever approach that pays off big time. While it's usually not a wise course of action to name-drop Roman poets and compare yourself to their epic heroes, Alex somehow manages to do it without appearing conceited. Perhaps she's successful because the comparison is followed by a rant that firmly establishes credibility as a first-class language geek. That's not intended as an insult: Alex effectively conveys her passion to the reader who is left with the impression that she reads the *Aeneid* the way other kids read Harry Potter. Her comparison isn't a pompous boast so much as a heartfelt identification with a beloved character.

Her first paragraph is the strongest. Alex not only quickly and effectively sets the scene, but also manages to draw the reader in to her state of mind, effectively leading into what's to come. The essay also has great flow. While the refrain, "If only . . ." smacks of high school angst, it keeps the reader moving along and ties together all of the thoughts presented.

It would have been nice if the introductory scene had played a larger role in the essay. The line in the penultimate paragraph about Velcro was a nice little connecting thread between the story she's telling and the point she's making. Sprinkling similar details throughout the piece would have polished up an already great essay.

The most effective part of this essay, though, would have to be the way Alex infused her voice into it. Her inner monologue is charming and her enthusiasm contagious. She is really herself in this essay.

—Zach T. Osborn

DAVID LIU

It was a typical midsummer evening, hot and humid. The air hung stagnant, pressing on me like a thick blanket. . . .

Bam!

The gunshot lingered in the heavy air for an instant. Then nearly ninety thousand people began screaming. I was one of them.

The journey that brought me to this moment had been long.

It began in elementary school. At the time, I had a youthful confidence in my running skills, even entertaining the idea of participating at the Olympics one day. The tough competition of high school, however, brought me back to earth. Going to the Olympics was clearly not within my reach, and that particular ambition was reluctantly relegated to a dusty corner of my consciousness.

Later, in a moment of inspiration, I rekindled the flame of that old dream—could I possibly volunteer to work for the United States at the 2008 Beijing Summer Olympics? At first, I enthusiastically attempted to sign up as a volunteer for the track team. After being summarily rejected because of my young age, for a brief moment I felt as if my hopes were doomed to be snuffed out again. Unwilling to accept defeat, I regrouped and realized that my most useful quality—Chinese fluency—would best serve the Media Services department. While Bob Condron, head of that branch, was more open to my request, he remained hesitant (I would only be sixteen at the time of the Games). Undeterred, I suggested using the volunteering experience as part of my Eagle Scout project, which rules state must be completed before my eighteenth birthday. To my great joy, Mr. Condron soon accepted me as a member of their team, adding, "We've never hired an underage volunteer in the U.S. Olympic Committee before. "

However, there were still daunting obstacles barring the way to Beijing. Chief among these was cost—as a volunteer, I had to pay for everything, and since my mother had to accompany me (an unfortunate consequence of being underage), we were in need of quite a bit of cash. To raise the necessary funds, I sought out work, eventually gaining experience in an eclectic group of occupations. I also fund-raised extensively, describing myself and my project at a number of companies and organizations. While this was difficult, it gave me practice in speaking to a number of people from different backgrounds.

As you've undoubtedly realized, the opening scenario isn't the latest script for an exciting crime/drama TV series, but it was arguably even more thrilling. Exactly 19.3 seconds after that gunshot, Usain Bolt broke the twelve-year-old world record in the 200-meter sprint.

As I walked out of the stadium, I was lost in thought: lost in the history I bore witness to, and lost in everything I had experienced to get to that point. How fortunate I was, to have learned to forge ahead in all circumstances, finding alternative approaches when necessary. How fortunate I was, to have the stars align so seamlessly—my love for sports and Chinese meshed perfectly with the Olympics that just happened to be hosted in China. How fortunate I was, to be able to seize that opportunity. Best of all, how fortunate I *am*, to accomplish my childhood dream.

The chatter of thousands of jubilant fans jolted me from my reverie. I took a deep breath, quickened my pace, and joined them as we headed to the bus stop.

REVIEW

David begins his essay with an unusual and very successful hook. Unlike similar openings that start with a dramatic scene, he uses the ambiguity of language to his benefit. The red herring he creates when describing the gunshot both cleverly twists a preexisting mental image and creates a mystery about the connection between events that slowly reveal themselves throughout the essay. It is an effective rhetorical tool that compels the admissions officer to keep reading.

The international experience is the most obvious, and often most envied, choice for the college essay. It is seen as the easiest way to get the attention of the admissions committee and demonstrate the unique background you would bring to the school that is always mentioned in admissions' presentations. What David does very well, though, is place the experience within the context of its personal significance. He effectively communicates how he developed a personal goal and worked hard to achieve it, but the real strength of the essay comes from the last two paragraphs. David captures a moment in time and then connects all of the various themes he has developed throughout the essay, from the opening hook to his own previous achievements. Clearly a very skilled writer, he uses visual imagery to reflect on the circumstances around him. In the process, he provides key insights into his individual personality and his ability to appreciate and learn from a particular experience.

Of course, there are aspects of the essay he could improve. The paragraph in which David details how he landed a volunteer spot with the team, in particular, reads more like a professional cover letter than a personal recollection on perseverance. On the whole, however, David has written a masterful essay that can provide a model for narrative structures within a college essay.

—Raul P. Quintana

VI. PASSION

Writing about something important to you can go a long way in a personal statement. The essays in this section describe something the author is passionate about, and they are generally successful. This can be a great medium to demonstrate why a school should admit you and what you'll do with your education. Showing passion for something—be it academics, an extracurricular, or a way of thinking—reassures the admissions office that you are more than a résumé.

But with that in mind, it is important to make sure that essays do demonstrate passion successfully; otherwise, they come off as half-hearted excuses for listing accomplishments and abilities—a huge turnoff in a personal essay.

Also, remember that most people are not as passionate as you are about your topic. When writing about a passion, you have to not only sell yourself, but also the thing you are describing. Generally, if you care enough about your topic, this sentiment will show through, making this class of essays a strong choice for the personal statement. The focus of the essay can remain on you while you can describe something simpler than the entirety of who you are as a person.

YE ZHAO

The first principle is that you must not fool yourself—and
you are the easiest person to fool.

—Richard Phillips Feynman,
Caltech commencement address, 1974

The closing ceremony started. One after another, participants went
up the stage to receive what were deserving of us. I had gotten a bronze
medal. It was not too bad considering that it was my first time in such
a competition.

"Now for the special awards," the emcee announced. "The best
female participant for the Asian Physics Olympiad 2008 is Ye Zhao
from Singapore."

The audience broke into rapturous applause, leaving me in a pleas-
ant surprise. Quickly, I was prompted to go up the stage. I felt honored and even delighted. Getting top for something in an international
competition should be quite an achievement; my parents and teachers
will be very proud of me. Off the stage, other female participants came
over to congratulate me, albeit with a tad of envy. My very frank fellow
male Singapore participant who has gotten gold in the same competition joked:

"I have gotten gold. Yet *you* are given a nice trophy and a camera
when you got bronze. It is all because that you are a girl."

It was all because that I am a girl. My spirit sank. The crystal trophy suddenly became heavy. It was like a hammer pounding my heart.

The issue of gender never concerned me until then. Being brought
up in a coeducational school where boys and girls did equally well in

class, I never really felt that guys are in anyway superior to their female counterparts. However, this time, I felt a pinch in my heart. I felt that we are not quite on the same footing after all (for physics at least). They are guys. We are girls.

Special awards are set up for the females in Physics Olympiads because people feel that girls will not perform as well as boys in physics. Though I believe that there is no inherent difference between the genders, I witnessed the differences between the performance of males and females in the subject. In my Physics Honors class, among the participants for the Olympiads and for any physics faculty in university, there are a disproportionately small percentage of females.

In the midst of all the chattering from the participants, I was thrown into deep thought. The award was set up to encourage girls in physics and yet is a stark reminder of the perceived "intellectual" gap between males and females. What impression does it leave behind for females who aspire for the pinnacle of the field? What mark will such reminders make in the subconscious of little girls who might have wanted to fiddle around with machines alongside their brothers?

I finally accepted the award with much ambivalence and even a tinge of regret. But then, I knew there is no other sensible thing to do without creating a big fuss. The trophy now serves as a reminder, not of an achievement but of a duty. I will strive to be a role model female physicist. And I will work toward the day when all will find special awards of this sort unnecessary. Whether female or male, I believe that with our love for physics, we can excel in the field equally.

REVIEW

Ye writes a very compelling narrative that displays her talent for physics as well as her social awareness and determination to be a leader in her field. Her writing style is very direct and easy for the reader to understand. Despite the occasional instances of awkward syntax, Ye remains an effective narrator who lets the reader into a defining moment of her life.

Ye's narration of the award ceremony demonstrates her personal growth and maturity to the admissions committee. Most people may write about an award ceremony as an end point to show their hard work and accomplishments, but to Ye it was a learning point and moment of profound realization. The readers are able to grasp her emotions as she effectively conveys the weight of the words, "It is all because that you are a girl."

In this moment, Ye is able to uncover a subtle paradox: The existence of the special award for girls clearly acknowledges a gender gap. As she tells the reader about her previous observations of gender inequality, she maintains a conversational yet persuasive tone, conveying a sense of urgency. Thus the reader cannot help but see the importance of the issue and want to support girls like Ye who "might have wanted to fiddle around with machines alongside their brothers." Although Ye herself clearly excels in the field, the reader perceives her social consciousness and awareness of the barriers that other girls may face.

Overall, Ye portrays herself as an accomplished female who realizes her unique position and wants to bring equal opportunity in physics to all females. In her drive to be "a role model female physicist," Ye shows great promise as a passionate leader who will empower other females and share her dedication with her classmates at Harvard.

—Michelle S. Lee

Octav Dragoi

A light breeze caressing the cornfield makes it look like a gentle sway-ing sea of gold under the ginger sun of late summer. A child's chime-like laughter echoes. As I rush through the cornfield, I hear the rustling of leaves and the murmur of life hidden among the stems that tower over me.

I remember the joy of the day when I solved one of my first difficult combinatorics problems at my parents' house in the countryside. I felt so exhilarated that I ran outside and into the cornfield. As I was pass-ing row after row of stems, I realized the cornfield was actually a giant matrix with thousands of combinations of possible pathways, just like the combinatorics problem I had just solved. I looked at the sky and I thought about the great mathematicians of the past that contributed so much to this field and about how I have added yet another dimen-sion to my matrix. Suddenly, mathematics appeared to me as a 3D live map where staggering arrays of ideas connect each other by steady flows of sheer wisdom.

Suddenly a loud laughter from the next room wakes me up from my reverie. I am back in my room in the drab dormitory where I lived since I was fifteen. The dim sunset barely lightens up my room, while the cold November wind rushes from the broken-and-mended-with-tape window on the hallway, whistling beneath my door. My room-mates haven't returned yet, and I feel alone and isolated.

In moments such as these I always take out the ultimate weapon against gloominess: the picture of my family. I look at myself, my par-ents, my little sister, and my grandfather at the countryside, under a clear blue sky, hugging, sharing the joy of being together. It reminds me of the old times, when life was simpler, but it also reminds me of why I came to Bucharest to live in a dormitory. It was because mathematics fascinated me with its beautiful and intricate theories and configurations, and my parents and my family supported me 150 percent. They put in long hours at work to pay for school costs and they selflessly accepted my long absences. I decided then to honor their support, follow our common dream, and become an accomplished mathematician.

Finally today I consider I matched at least an infinitesimal part of my parents' work. After countless Olympiad stages and fierce selection programs, I managed to win a gold medal at the International Mathematical Olympiad, along with scoring what is called "an ace": getting gold medals in the National Olympiad, the Balkan Olympiad, and the International Olympiad.

Math, for me, is a vast map of knowledge where theories intersect each other like pathways in a cornfield, and that explains the laws of nature and the universe itself. However, no matter what mathematical sphere shall I soar in, I will always have my family with me and the joy of that day when I was running freely in the cornfield.

REVIEW

Octav wrote a very touching essay that does the impossible: speaks to the importance of math and family in his life at once without ever drifting into a realm of deep sentimentality. The use of such excellent and artistic prose to describe such a potentially monotonous subject allows the writing to show Octav's depth.

But he does digress into a step-by-step description of his mathematical achievements, which are included elsewhere in his application. His love of math speaks to the passion he wants to express to a reader. The gold medals he's won indicate others' perceptions of him—not something particularly relevant to this personal statement. He seems to think that these facts are important parts of the description of his relationship with math. In reality, he nearly loses the reader, giving the impression that his interest in math stems from external praise.

But in the end, this essay makes Octav seem like an extremely talented applicant without coming off as too self-promoting. His dual focus on his future career and his love of family demonstrate his balanced personality, and he convinces the reader that his love of math is genuine.

—Amy Friedman

JOSHUAH CAMPBELL

My Something

Jeremiah and I have a lot in common; the one from the Bible, I mean, that comes before Lamentations and after Isaiah. God sent Jeremiah on a mission at a young age; He gave him an assignment that he could not turn down. I'm young, seventeen years old, and, like Jeremiah, I was at first unsure about my assignment. However, on August 28, I stood before my congregation and announced my intent to preach a sermon on trial. Never since had I felt the strange combination of relief and nausea that I felt at that moment. It was then that I was finally sure, sure that the inner pull that I had been feeling for the past four years was not due to stress-induced indigestion. The strangest sensation I have ever felt is knowing that I am supposed to be doing something, and not know what that *something* is. Now, I've found my *something*, the *something* God had in store for me.

Words cannot describe what it's like to be a child who does not fit in, not because of some disability, or because of some undesirable trait, but because he has a calling on his life. Little did I know that, even in my earliest years, God was shaping me into the *something* He wanted my life to be. It is at the same time humbling and terrifying to think that God chose me before he "formed [me] in the womb." To be honest, I find it hard to believe that He found me that important. My parents are not super-Christians; my father definitely isn't a priest like Jeremiah's father. Still, He chose *me,* and it's even more frightening to realize that "Why me?" is a question I may never be able to answer. But, like Jeremiah, I didn't have much of a choice. God wanted Jeremiah just as He wants me, and I can either choose obedience or a life lacking fulfillment.

As it happened, I couldn't use the "too young" excuse, either. Jeremiah tried that one, and God's response was: "Do not say, 'I am only a youth,' for you will go to everyone I send you to and speak whatever I tell you. Do not be afraid of anyone, for I will be with you to deliver you." To be honest again, when I stand behind the pulpit next year, I am going to be scared, shaken to my core because of the gravity of the task I must carry out. I know that already. Jeremiah knew it, too. The good news is so does God, which is why He filled Jeremiah's mouth with His words. I hope He'll do the same for me.

In the end, all the people who knew I'd be a preacher one day were right. Yes, I still plan to have fun in college, and, no, I really don't want to pastor a congregation. I just want to be like Jeremiah, to be the *something* God wants me to be.

REVIEW

Joshuah's essay is striking in its description of his dedication to God—though, as he describes, his parents are not "super-Christians," Joshuah feels a very strong connection to his religion. This is a foreign feeling to many readers, but Joshuah recognizes this possibility and is careful to describe not just a dedication to God that may not make sense to some, but the way that dedication makes him feel—emotions that anyone can relate to.

Joshuah also avoids the common trap of centering an essay on something other than oneself. Often, essays about important figures in one's life—parents, grandparents, good friends—convince an admissions officer that the person *described* is a wonderful human being, but do little for the applicant's case. In this instance, Joshuah describes his feelings toward God, but still keeps the story about himself.

This well-crafted essay does everything a personal statement should do: It gives the reader a sense of the applicant as a person and it demonstrates Joshuah's ability to write coherently and cohesively, while also maintaining the originality the best essays need to stand out.

—Indrani G. Das

SADIE McQUILKIN

For every step I take, I could list a dozen reasons why I run. But most of all, I run because I couldn't.

Maybe it was the sixteen-mile run at a breakneck pace the week before. Maybe it was the impromptu dip into the icy Atlantic Ocean immediately following the run. Maybe it was the residual stress from midyear exams. Maybe I was just going too fast down the ski slope that fateful day last January. Regardless of what precise combination of factors preceded it, the outcome was the same: The anterior crucial ligament in my left knee was destroyed, along with any hope I had of completing my first marathon in the spring.

In the months before my ski accident, running had consumed the majority of my thoughts, energy, and time. I had stopped saying, "I run," and instead had begun to proudly declare, "I'm a runner." My shift in syntax reflected my intensity and devotion to training. When a simple indiscretion stole my ability to run, it took with it a major part of my identity. Preparing for a marathon had empowered me to define myself on my own terms, to take charge of my own life. Being deprived of my goal forced me to redefine my concept of self and success. The sense of failure that began to sink in after my injury was far more painful than any physical symptom. The dull ache in my knee following surgery—and even the excruciating stab of a blood clot—paled in comparison to my emotional turmoil.

Not until I acknowledged my misery was I able to take the first step toward regaining my identity. I realized that the fatalistic pessimism into which I had allowed myself to sink did not reflect how I normally perceived myself or how others characterized me. No, I was—and always will be—the one to seek a positive perspective in any situation. By the time I returned to school eight days after my knee operation, I was determined to face my daily challenges with a smile on my face and a spring in my step—even if my gait was more of a limp than a skip. I refused to pity myself, and instead focused my energy on experiencing the present to the fullest possible extent.

My unplanned hiatus from running last winter allowed me to examine how I value and allocate my time. I realized that running was not the sole source of satisfaction in my life; even if I couldn't improve my mile splits, I could become a better friend, sister, and daughter. Prior to tearing my ACL, the whirlwind speeds at which I had been living my life had left me little time to focus on anyone but myself. My injury forced me to slow down and appreciate all of the people in my life who offered me so much support. I learned to focus more of my energy on taking care of the people I love, and in the process, prevented myself from slipping into self-pity. Getting a friend to laugh or providing a shoulder to cry on became just as fulfilling for me as finishing a race. Though my muscles atrophied, my relationships grew in strength and depth.

Now, as I ease my way back into cross-country season, the sport feels both comfortably familiar and entirely new. The physical motions are the same, but my emotions regarding running have changed. I no longer run to fulfill expectations I have constructed for myself; I run because I want to show my teammates that I love running as much I love them. I run because it makes me stronger—physically, mentally, and emotionally. Ultimately, I run because I can.

REVIEW

This essay creatively uses an injury as a vehicle for a discussion of the perseverance and positivity possessed by the author. One of its greatest strengths is the work's framing. Beginning with answering the question of "Why do I run?" the essay catches the reader's attention and continues on to discuss possible answers. One of these answers develops into a discussion of the injury that the essay centers on. The natural flow set up by this sequence continues as the conclusion brings readers full circle, offering a final answer to the question posed in the introduction.

At first glance, Sadie's essay is about overcoming obstacles. She was injured and needed to recover. But it falls into the Passion section because, in the end Sadie did not overcome the obstacle, she embraced it. She allowed it to shape and help her understand her passion for running. Unlike the earlier essay about running to overcome obstacles, Sadie does not conclude with a personal-best race—the prime example of outward success. She instead concludes with an internal success, and to great effect.

The essay is a work to be proud of. Upon the ending readers feel the message is complete and have a favorable sense of the author's personality and passion.

—Juliet Nelson

WILL SHIH

I suppose there are some trade-offs when you dedicate yourself to becoming the best debater you can be. The first weekend of Spring Break is always the IHSA State Debate Tournament. After progressing from not placing as a freshman to being a semifinalist as a sophomore, my partner Jeff and I were hungry for a state championship. It was also our last chance. Jeff was a year older and he was graduating.

The whole night, we stayed up preparing, honing the wording of our speeches, looking for new evidence to refute others, and coming up with creative arguments that would hopefully surprise our opponents. Our ace in the hole was an argument that we had written based on the Arab Spring destabilizing Bahrain and threatening our Navy's 5th Fleet there. As we were monitoring the situation using Google News to ensure the situation didn't change too much, our teammate John burst into the room, iPad in hand, with the news that the French had just green-lighted air strikes on Libya. After Jeff and John stopped their research to debate the merits of NATO action in Libya, I tried in vain to refocus them, urging them to help me finish our work so we could go to bed. Eventually I succumbed to my own desire to join the debate and we all huddled around John's iPad to watch the CNN report on the Libyan bombings.

After about three hours of sleep, we put on our suits and ties and checked one final time on the situation in Bahrain. We ended up at the same round in which we had lost the previous year, the semifinal round, with the Bahrain argument still in our back pocket. It worked to perfection and we moved on to the final. Despite losing there to a nationally ranked New Trier team, we came home with a towering trophy and we noticed that despite the fact that it said RUNNER-UP, our trophy was just as big as the first-place trophy. As we sat at Panera, finally relaxing after a stretch of three days when I slept about ten hours total, I began to realize how much debate has changed me.

Debate has taught me how to tie a tie and which buttons to button on a suit. I've been motivated to open my eyes and find research like Professor Devah Pager's study that says a white felon has an equal or better chance at getting a job as a black man with no criminal record. I've been exposed to the ideas of Malthus and Sun Tzu. I know more about the threat of a nuclear electromagnetic pulse (EMP) attack than any sane seventeen-year-old should know. I can't even watch an advertisement without thinking about all the fallacies in their argumentation.

I thought then about what my friends and classmates had probably done that first weekend of Spring Break. I looked around at my teammates, leaned over to Jeff and said, "There's no other place I'd rather be right now."

And he replied, "Yeah, me neither."

REVIEW

In this essay, Will writes about his experience in high school debate—specifically, he addresses the many lessons and knowledge he has gained, as well as the sacrifices he had to make.

Although the topic of the essay is rather standard, the strength lies in the way he frames and structures the story. With a very clear beginning, middle, and end, the essay is easy to follow and shows the author's dedication and passion for debate. A lot of applicants are discouraged from writing about common topics, such as high school debate or sports, but as long as the essay itself is able to illuminate something new and insightful, the topic of the essay matters far less than the content and the way the story is depicted.

Will's essay has its shortfalls as well. First, while the description of the Arab Spring in the second paragraph is helpful in building context, it is unnecessarily detailed and therefore distracting to the whole flow of the essay.

But when he isn't lost in detail, Will presents a complete picture of how debate has changed him as a person, and his deep interest in this activity speaks positively to his character, and his use of subtle humor ties his essay together cleanly and elegantly.

—Jane Seo

James Gillette

There are few classes I would choose to repeat even once, let alone twice. I would hate to do so not necessarily because I hated the class, but rather because it would be the same experience and the same content over again. However this was not the case with journalism.

I applied to be a part of the newspaper staff on a whim at the end of my freshman year and was surprised to find out that I'd made it. I spent that summer questioning what being on staff would mean. Mostly I was wondering how much work would be involved. When I returned to East that fall I was hit over the head with my sophomore year workload. Instead of hating how difficult it was to get quote verification forms signed or how our copy/source editor was super intense, I found myself really enjoying the class. By the end of the year I noticed the impact journalism had already had on me—I was a much stronger writer, a more confident conversationalist, and a much more informed individual. The paper mattered to me, so I signed up for a second year and was pleasantly surprised when I was promoted to Arts & Entertainment Editor.

I found my second year in journalism to be remarkably different. With different people in charge and lots of new writers I felt the nudge to take some responsibility. Wanting to create a positive experience for younger writers, I did my best to emulate the better editors from the previous year by being approachable, knowledgeable, and helpful. I discovered I have a knack for creating "artsy" layouts, and a way with the outmoded computers we use. I became more of a general editor for any confused reporters and the tech guy (meaning I could use a scanner and knew some hotkey commands). Naturally I still felt a strong tie to this periodical and I again registered to be on staff for my senior year. I was surprised and excited to learn that I had been named Editor-in-Chief for 2011 to 2012.

In anticipation of the coming year I spent the summer updating the staff policies and contacting local printers to investigate switching from our old one (with whom we'd developed some issues). To prepare myself as a leader I attended a National Scholastic Press Association editorial workshop at the University of Minnesota. There I learned management skills, received a critique of our paper, and compared our work to that of other high schools in the Midwest. This workshop gave me some great ideas for updating and improving our paper. For example, for years we have used Microsoft Publisher, which is a difficult program to work with. That August, I purchased Adobe InDesign for the class laptop and taught myself to use the program.

So far this year has been a year of great change for *The Greyhound*. I've switched our printing partner, changed the paper type to actual newsprint, radically updated our layout, upgraded our programs and technology, added color printing, cut production costs by 40 to 50 percent, and improved our production cycle to help writers rather than pressure them.

The newspaper has helped me develop as a leader and as a student and it has given me a great sense of accomplishment. I am proud to have been a part of its staff for three years. Each year brought new people, new ideas, and new perspectives for me. What had been an almost reluctant application resulted in one of my best high school experiences.

REVIEW

In this essay, the author discusses his years of experience in journalism and involvement in the school newspaper to describe how he has grown as a leader. The details he discusses about his work on his newspaper are interesting and help to build the picture of a dedicated, hardworking student.

But though James demonstrates his ability to write a decent story with clear, descriptive language, he commits one major error. Strikingly, James's essay reads awfully like a list of accomplishments. Though the context he introduces makes his successes more personable, the essay is never about James as a person, but rather is about what he has done on the newspaper. This essay is appropriate for the part of the application that requests extra information on extracurriculars, but is not as revealing as it could be. He uses a simplistic, chronological structure to tell a fairly mundane story, and with it fails to demonstrate creativity.

With that said, individually the paragraphs, accomplishments, and lessons learned are quite interesting, and often use relevant details to create a vivid scene. He details the way he grows over the years, demonstrating his ability to adapt and change as adaptation and change are demanded of him. While we may not get the best idea of who James is at the moment, he is clearly moving toward more dynamic pursuits and larger challenges.

—Jane Seo

CONNOR DENNEY

As a child, I was entranced with tales of questing and adventure. I enjoyed reading about journeys fraught with peril undertaken for a noble goal. Unfortunately, I would have to be content with merely reading legends of knights and maidens, treasure hunters, or ring-bearing hobbits. I knew that I could never have an adventure as inspiring as those I found in books.

It was soon after this acknowledgment that my father introduced my family to geocaching. Called the "Great American GPS Stash Hunt" for a reason, this game quickly stole my heart. Geocaching, which involves using a GPS to find containers hidden in public by other "geocachers" who post the objects' coordinates online, was the quest for which I had been searching. It was my way to become a Sir Galahad. Not caring for the tiny McDonald's toys found in most geocaches, I lived for the hunt; it was not the Holy Grail that enticed me, but the challenge of finding it.

This activity has served as a sightseeing tool on vacations, giving us tours of cities around the world as we troop through on our adventures. I imagine myself to be Juan Ponce de León looking for the Fountain of Youth. On coastal hunts I am Captain Kidd. In cities I am James Bond or Jason Bourne. Geocaching has allowed me to transcend the monotony of real life; it has granted me the adventures I have yearned for.

As I entered high school, my free time seemed to vanish overnight. I devoted more time to studies and athletic practices, leaving little opportunity to enjoy the hobby that I enjoyed so much. I savored the rare occasions when I could geocache with my family without scholastic stress. However, geocaching remained an integral part of my life, be it in a metaphorical sense. The physical quest for a film canister or Altoid tin was replaced with a quest for knowledge. I immersed myself in studies not only for my high school classes, but in fields above and beyond the level of my education. I found myself searching for El Dorado in mathematical essays and websites; I slew the dragon of ignorance by reading *Time* and hosting political debates on Facebook. Though I would rarely embark on geocaching hunts, I became a geocacher for knowledge.

This pursuit has altered my viewpoint on school. Whereas I had previously considered it a place to learn from books and to achieve high grades, I began to search for information outside of class curriculum. School became a training ground, my Camelot, a castle where I could learn the basic skills of attaining knowledge and wisdom before embarking on my journey in the real world. Whether I will be able to find time to geocache later in life or not, I will always be affected by the game that satisfied my lust for adventure and influenced my desire to learn.

REVIEW

Connor writes about a hobby that is truly unusual—geocaching. He enthusiastically explains the hobby thoroughly enough for the reader to understand, which makes his unusual pastime an excellent choice for a paper topic. Geocaching becomes a clever metaphor for Connor's transformation, which gives the reader a better sense of his academic motivation.

The reader becomes more familiar with Connor's personality and motivations as a result of his interconnected stories. Leading off with a familiar example—like fairy tales and adventure novels—helps prepare the reader for the introduction of geocaching, the piece's central metaphor. After explaining what geocaching is, Connor then moves away from the activity itself and focuses on how the key features of his hobby can apply to other areas of his life. His transition from the physical activity to his metaphorical treatment of it is clear enough as to not confuse readers, but its lack of nuance is a disservice to the essay. Though broadening the focus of his paper to include more than just his interest in a part-time hobby is a good decision, the relationship he draws is a little overdone though his enthusiasm for both carry him quite far in an essay that brings out his personality and character. They both come through in the essay in a way that is highly beneficial for his application, but he falls flat when trying to generalize his geocaching hobby to his academic pursuits.

—Charlotte D. Smith

ANUMITA DAS

I am a messenger.

I scan the expanse before me. Three hundred eighth graders stare at me expectantly. The headmasters of Boston Latin School wait patiently from their canvases on the walls. Rows of lightbulbs shine faithfully from the ceiling, illuminating the hall. I lower my chin, glancing momentarily at the wooden floors, and close my eyes. When I look up, I see multitudes of men prostrated across the ground in worship. I hear thousands of voices echoing the praises of God. I have become Elie Wiesel in the concentration camp of Buna, and I speak my thoughts aloud.

"Why, but why, should I bless him? In every fiber I rebelled."

I see the heavy billows of smoke from incinerators. I watch in horror as men become ravenous beasts for a morsel of food. An irrepressible anger surges in my own fibers—anger at God, who is unmoved by the suffering of humankind. Yet on this Rosh Hashanah, men continue to chant the Kaddish in His honor. People still wish one another a "Happy New Year" in the confines of this prison camp. I realize that man has emerged the stronger. Man has triumphed.

In my lifetime of only seventeen years, I have already undergone nearly twenty transformations like this one. I have been Susan B. Anthony, Anne Frank, and Netaji Subhash Chandra Bose among others since I started Public Declamation in eighth grade. As a declaimer, five times a year, I select and memorize a piece to present to an audience of hundreds of students, but there is more to declamation than memorizing and reciting. Declamation is a process of internalizing—of learning and understanding.

Passion

I can read *Night*. I can read it to my mother. I could probably even memorize it and recite it to myself in front of a mirror. But when I declaim *Night*, something happens to me. I experience a profound metamorphosis—a gut-level identification with Elie Wiesel beyond the text. I am changed. His emotions become my own emotions, his thoughts my own. His strength becomes the source of my own strength. I am Elie Wiesel.

As I walk off the stage that day having declaimed an excerpt from *Night*, I remember the day that I learned from Susan B. Anthony to assert my beliefs and never let anyone deny me my rights. I remember the day I learned from Anne Frank to see the bright side of situations and to appreciate the small pleasures taken for granted in life. I remember the day I learned from Netaji Subhash Chandra Bose what it means to be devoted to one's country. And I realize that it is my duty to share these messages, to preserve them and to remember them—I am not only a declaimer. I am a messenger.

REVIEW

Anumita's essay describes how the act of declaiming transcends mere memorization and delivery and puts her in the shoes of the original speaker. In doing so Anumita in turn puts the reader into her shoes and brings her experience to life with vivid imagery and simple but elegant prose. Anumita transitions seamlessly from an illustration of declaiming to its effects on her and how it has informed her life philosophy—the essay flows smoothly from one paragraph to the next and maintains the reader's interest throughout. By choosing to relate the impact of a broad experience—in this case, declamation—through several examples rather than focusing on a single, defining moment, Anumita more effectively illustrates the ways in which declamation has changed her and allows the reader to accompany her on the journey of her development.

This essay is strong in almost every respect. It is extremely well organized: The intriguing introduction is followed by a brief but necessary orienting explanation, after which Anumita discusses in more detail the uniqueness of declamation and the correspondingly unique impact it has had on her. Each section fits perfectly into the essay as a whole, which is concise and eloquently written. It reads almost like a speech in and of itself, adding yet another dimension to what is already a wonderfully powerful narrative. A particularly impressive feature of this essay is its ability to be striking but not overpowering: The abrupt switch from an ordinary school hall to a concentration camp in the introduction is somehow captivating rather than confusing. Overall, this is an incredibly well-written essay that provides insight into not only the significance of declamation but also Anumita's personality and her gift for storytelling.

—Christina M. Teodorescu

VII. INSPIRATION

Essays, about inspiration are common enough that authors should take care to avoid what has become a bit of a cliché for admissions officers. The formulaic essay reads as follows: Author meets someone worse off than him- or herself; author realizes that he or she has done nothing to merit an easier life; author decides to use the lessons learned to fix the world in the future. Writing an essay that doesn't stand out defeats the purpose of the personal statement. After reading your essay, admissions officers should know you and remember you, and a bland essay won't accomplish that.

The repetitive and unoriginal insights aren't the only things to watch out for when writing an essay about inspiration. Often, essays of this nature attempt to sum up the whole of a student's inspirations in one five-hundred-word piece. For most, this is an impossible task, and the end result is unfocused. The good essays of this nature focus on one source of inspiration and delve deeply into the author's relationship with it.

Though they can go wrong, these essays can also be a great medium for a student to show dedication to a cause. The idea of admitting the next leader of UNICEF or the person who will cure juvenile rheumatoid arthritis is appealing to an admissions officer, and if an essay successfully conveys an applicant's dedication to that cause, it could be a great selling point.

ANTHONY WILDER WOHNS

Tsunamis, Garlic, and One Thousand Cranes

I had never seen houses floating down a river. Minutes before there had not even been a river. An immense wall of water was destroying everything in its wake, picking up fishing boats to smash them against buildings. It was the morning of March 11, 2011. Seeing the images of destruction wrought by the earthquake and tsunami in Japan, I felt as if something within myself was also being shaken, for I had just spent two of the happiest summers of my life there.

In the summer of my freshman year, I received the Kikkoman National Scholarship, which allowed me to travel to Japan to stay with a host family in Tokyo for ten weeks. I arrived just as the swine flu panic gripped the world, so I was not allowed to attend high school with my host brother, Yamato. Instead, I took Japanese language, judo, and karate classes and explored the confusing sprawl of the largest city in the world. I spent time with the old men of my neighborhood in the *onsen*, or hot spring, questioning them about the Japan of their youth. They laughed and told me that if I wanted to see for myself, I should work on a farm.

The next summer I returned to Japan, deciding to heed the old men's advice and volunteer on a farm in Japan's northernmost island, Hokkaido. I spent two weeks working more than fourteen hours a day. I held thirty-pound bags of garlic with one hand while trying to tie them to a rope hanging from the ceiling with the other, but couldn't hold the bags in the air long enough. Other days were spent pulling up endless rows of *daikon*, or Japanese radish, which left rashes on my arms that itched for weeks. Completely exhausted, I stumbled back to the farmhouse, only to be greeted by the family's young children who were eager to play. I passed out every night in a room too small for me to straighten my legs. One day, I overslept a lunch break by two hours. I awoke mortified, and hurried to the father. After I apologized in the most polite form of Japanese, his face broke into a broad grin. He patted me on the back and said, "You are a good worker, Anthony. There is no need to apologize." This single exchange revealed the true spirit of the Japanese farmer. The family had lived for years in conditions that thoroughly wore me out in only a few days. I had missed two hours of work, yet they were still perpetually thankful to me. In their life of unbelievable hardship, they still found room for compassion.

When I had first gone to Tokyo, I had sought the soul of the nation among its skyscrapers and urban hot springs. The next summer I spurned the beaten track in an attempt to discover the true spirit of Japan. While lugging enormously heavy bags of garlic and picking *daikon*, I found that spirit. The farmers worked harder than anyone I have ever met, but they still made room in their hearts for me. So when the tsunami threatened the people to whom I owed so much, I had to act. Remembering the lesson of compassion I learned from the farm family, I started a fund-raiser in my community called "One Thousand Cranes for Japan." Little more than two weeks later, we had raised over $8,000 and a flock of one thousand cranes was on its way to Japan.

REVIEW

The prompt to which this essay responds—*discuss some issue of personal, local, national, or international concern and its importance to you*—is by far, the most difficult to pull off. Students who choose to craft their essays around this or similar prompts have a tendency to drown out experiences conveyed in their own voices with universal accepted truths expressed on behalf of the masses. Remember, the goal here is to write a personal statement—not to draft a global Bill of Rights.

Approach this essay as you would a photomontage: The trick to using the prompt as successfully as Anthony is to properly adjust the camera's zoom. Anthony begins his essay with a landscape of the tsunami, and then zooms in to end on a vivid portrait of his own character. Essentially, Anthony uses the tsunami to frame the story of his life rather than using his life as a backdrop for a discussion about the tsunami.

The crowning achievement of Anthony's essay is the subtlety with which it illustrates Anthony's compassion and humanitarian spirit. The true subject of Anthony's essay is not the tsunami, not the time Anthony spent in Japan, but his fund-raiser. Yet, Anthony limits his discussion of the charitable accomplishment to the last two sentences of his personal statement. By choosing to focus on *why* he organized the fund-raiser instead of the fund-raiser itself, Anthony is able to portray his personality to the reader in a humble, rather than self-congratulatory, tone.

Anthony does this in a truly praiseworthy manner, allowing his experiences to speak for themselves. Anthony does not have to tell the admissions officer that he is culturally curious—the fact that he heeded the old men's advice and returned to Japan to volunteer on a farm does that for him. Anthony does not have to explain that he is a dedicated worker—his mortification at having overslept and the sincerity with which he profusely apologized to the family does that for him. The appropriate framing of his charitable deed enables Anthony to tackle the most challenging prompt for a college essay with a piece that brilliantly showcases his personal connection to an international tragedy and offers deep insight into his individual character.

—Maddie Sewani

SHANG WANG

The Dollar Menu Epiphany

The other day, I was presented with a grave predicament. It was late afternoon and I was ravenous. I had missed lunch due to band lessons, and my stomach did not enjoy being ignored for ten hours. As I finished running errands for my mom, I noticed the local McDonald's ahead, and was drawn to it like . . . well, like a hungry guy is drawn to a restaurant. As I walked inside, Dollar Menu posters on the wall for the McDouble and the McChicken seized my attention. Both meals called out to me, each arguing for its superior delectability, making my mouth water in anticipation. However, I could not choose between the two courses. No, that day, I wanted both. I was so starved that I knew I could stomach both savory selections. So I strode boldly up to the counter, ordered both, and savored how the flavors of the McDouble and McChicken blended together to make one of the most satisfying meals I have ever enjoyed.

As I sat there with both orders easily devoured, I realized that this situation provided a perfect solution to a dilemma that had plagued my mind since the onset of college applications: What would my college major be? Ever since kindergarten, I had been gripped by the ideas (however vague they were) of both medicine and law. I guess the powers of healing and justice have always infatuated me. As the years passed, my fascination in both areas grew as I began to accumulate intimate knowledge of the human body and the legal system. In high school, my appetite for medicine and law became even more ferocious. My course schedule, extracurricular clubs, and even my summers were piled to the breaking point with activities concerning my two passions and I was able to stomach these "burdens" because my love for medicine and law made me invincible to fatigue. Yet, I had always thought that I would have to give up one of these passions in college. However, with this McDonald's experience, I began to realize that perhaps I could handle both, so long as I maintained my desire.

On the drive home, my thoughts blossomed into maturity. I thought how choosing a career in one field over the other would be as cruel as selecting a McDouble over a McChicken. I could not simply select one without filling myself with regret. Therefore, I decided right there to split my time in college between biology and political science, and to lay off the impossible choice of limiting myself to one passion until later down the road. I was not shying away from a tough decision, but was rather avoiding closing any doors of opportunity before they had been thoroughly tested. My dream to enjoy a perfect blend of my passions is becoming increasingly realistic with the growth of multidisciplinary fields today, and I do not wish to deprive myself of such a possibility with premature judgment. I know enormous amounts of energy will be needed to make my vision become reality, but as long as my desires for medicine and law do not wane, I know I can complete any journey I must undertake. Years from now, I look forward to enjoying a double meal at McDonald's (or perhaps some healthier alternative), while relishing a career that blends my two loves of medicine and law in perfect harmony.

REVIEW

Shang's essay is unconventional right from the beginning. A McDonald's Dollar Menu does not seem like the type of place for an epiphany, but Shang manages to tie his extravagant McDonald's lunch to his personal life in a humorous but genuine way. Though the writing is occasionally over-the-top—with phrases like "my thoughts blossomed into maturity" or "blends my two loves of medicine and law in perfect harmony"—there is no doubt that the author is passionate about these fields. After reading this essay, there is also little doubt that Shang knows what he wants to do with at least the first few years of college, and that assuredness is difficult to get across in an essay without sounding arrogant.

There is really only one line of argument in this essay, but it is a relief that the author does not waste page space trying to squeeze in his high school accomplishments. Shang mentions that he had filled his plate in high school with "activities concerning my two passions," but there are no forced references to specific club names or honors received. Because the goal of the essay is to convince the reader that Shang is a driven student who has two strong interests, the economical use of plotline and description draws attention to Shang's fluent writing and his apparent determination to study both biology and political science. The essay itself reflects Shang's ability to argue, and through the simple organization of his words, Shang reveals an important aspect of being a lawyer or a doctor—to cut right to the chase.

Shang also inserts subtle and amusing puns into his essay. He writes that his "appetite for medicine and law became even more ferocious," and that he looks forward to "relishing a career" that combines the two areas of study. So, while some would prefer to have their cheese on the side, Shang has served up an enjoyable essay.

—Virginia Marshall

AL I. DUISWIN

Invisible Neighbors

My community encompasses a broad spectrum of racial, religious, and economic diversity. I became more acquainted with what this really means last summer, when I volunteered with my school UNICEF club at the Sacred Heart Organization five miles from my home, helping to distribute school supplies to low-income families. I was appalled to see the lines of people wrapping around two city blocks; I had never imagined there were so many underprivileged families in my community.

While checking eligibility documents and registering families with schoolchildren, I had the opportunity to chat with two Guatemalan mothers in their early twenties, recently arrived to the States with two children each. Their husbands worked as day laborers two hours away in Stockton. With a fragmented family stretched across northern California, these young mothers went to their limits to make ends meet. I could only imagine their anxiety as they arrived at the center the previous night, with only a thermos of hot soup to keep themselves warm. They spoke of several young delinquents who made catcalls and verbally harassed them in the early morning, yet they continued to sit on that bench, determined to wait out the fear and cold in order to obtain essential supplies for their families. I took special care to pack extra crayons and colored pencils into their children's backpacks, as I could only vicariously experience their plight.

This fleeting experience—this conversation with aspiring, ambitious immigrants—juxtaposed the extremes of privilege and need in my community. It also led me to reevaluate my perception of the American Dream as humble, modest gains rather than miracle stories, such as striking an overnight rags-to-riches jackpot. As the son of middle-class skilled immigrants, I enjoy the relative comfort of a warm, supportive family with plenty of amenities to indulge in. However, I have realized that poverty and ambition lie only a few miles from my home. Thus, I feel proud to help disadvantaged community members improve their temporal circumstances through hard work, perseverance, and above all, hope.

As I consider a future career and my role in society, I will never forget these unseen people whose reticent needs are so inadequately addressed. One major issue concerning our nation is affordable health care for minority groups with limited access to medical facilities, mainly due to economic hardships. The state of California now mandates vaccinations for schoolchildren, stressing the dire need for maintaining public health. Seeing such a predicament in my local community has further piqued my interest in the fields of pathology and immunology as I hope to one day discover cost-effective treatment methods that would be accessible to all impoverished communities—not just in the United States, but internationally as well. This would be a testament to my dream of furthering UNICEF's goal of improving the welfare of women and children mired in poverty worldwide.

REVIEW

Al's essay takes the form of a personal mission statement, relating his hopes and goals to the reader. His essay is heartfelt, and it is clear that he is earnest in his concerns. But the overly ambitious scope of his writing is detrimental to the effect he is trying to achieve. In the space allotted to him, Al muses on the American Dream, poverty, vaccinations, affordable health care, and the plight of immigrant laborers. It's a lot of material to cover in such a short essay and none of these subjects receive a great deal of attention.

Inspiration

There's the seed of a terrific story in Al's encounter with the Guatemalan mothers and it could have benefited from expansion. This was a formative experience for him, and if he were to demonstrate why he would have an even more successful essay. What caused these women to tell Al their story? Why did they stand out from the others he saw that day? Why did their story resonate with him? A tighter focus on this or a similar moment could have granted the reader insight into Al as a person that simply isn't there in the piece as written.

In this essay, Al could have utilized the commonly spoken instruction—"show, don't tell." Integrating this story with the thoughts and feelings it inspired in him would have led to a stronger essay than the one he managed to produce. Still, the ambition is clearly there, and Al presents himself as an interesting and intelligent person who would be an excellent addition to Harvard.

—Zach T. Osborn

Maliza K.

Picture in your mind a rheumatoid arthritis patient. Let me guess: elderly woman, hair gray or graying, right? Eight and a half years ago, I would have had the exact same image in my own mind, but my life took a course that proves that there are rheumatoid arthritis patients who do not fall in the typical category.

During third grade, I was diagnosed with juvenile rheumatoid arthritis (JRA). I distinctly remember the day things changed. One day I was having the time of my childhood life, playing volleyball with friends at recess, and the next I was bedridden, unable to move without feeling excruciating pain. Needless to say, the sudden change was disconcerting as it would be for an eight-year-old, or anyone for that matter.

Although I now see how lucky it is that JRA is a manageable illness, my third-grade self was not as easily assured. The first thing that came to mind was "Why?" Why did simple everyday tasks suddenly cause me pain? So, I promptly did what I am sure is every doctor's worst nightmare: I turned to the Internet for information. As a third grader, there was only so much I could find out. My research extended about as far as a simple Google search could take me, but at that age, it was enough for me to just know that it was not life threatening. However, as I grew into my early high school years, I found myself wanting to know more about JRA's causes and treatments. Once again, I took to the Internet—this time with a more mature, Internet-savvy mind. Many alternative treatments had explanations regarding how they work, but my particular treatment plan did not. Instead of finding all the answers I sought, I was left wondering why taking six tiny tablets of methotrexate once a week managed to keep the pain at bay. Methotrexate's mechanism in JRA remains unknown and it is something that still occupies my mind.

Eight and a half years later after diagnosis, I have stopped taking methotrexate and am a few short steps away from an arthritis-free existence. However, for me, being diagnosed with JRA does not act as a hindrance, but instead propels me even further in my desire to pursue a career in the biomedical field. Every twinge of pain I feel essentially works to boost my motivation. This past summer rather than reading the research of other scientists on the Internet, I became the researcher as I worked in a lab in the National Institutes of Health Center for Cancer Research. Although my research was not related to my own illness, it still caught my interest because I knew it could help someone suffering a much more serious fate to understand what is going on within their body and what can be done to stop it. My research experience deepened my investment in understanding the "whys" of life from the molecular level all the way up to the whole-body impact. In my particular department of pediatric oncology, it was fairly obvious that not all the patients have the same happy ending that I am living, but it is this discrepancy that pushes me to challenge myself to someday provide real-world people with their own happy endings.

REVIEW

In her essay, Maliza explains the origins of her passion for research, drawing a connection between her childhood struggle with a debilitating disease and her experience working in a lab. The "overcoming obstacles" genre of college essays all too often falls into the trap of self-pity, but Maliza frankly and openly tells her story in a style that avoids self-indulgence entirely and brings to life a personality that is both optimistic and engaging. Her tone is refreshing in its simplicity and the essay reads almost like a conversational monologue, adding vitality to what could easily have been a five-hundred-word cliché.

The strengths of this essay lie in its skillful combination of powerful content and frank expression. Its weighty subject matter is balanced nicely by its casual style. Maliza brings her readers into her story from the very beginning, addressing them directly and encouraging them to challenge their preconceived notions of rheumatoid arthritis, as she had to do when confronted with the disease as a child. Her brief but vivid description of "the day things changed" introduces a surprisingly relatable narrative that successfully maintains the interest of the reader as it follows Maliza's journey toward research. The image of a third grader using Google to find information about her illness is an honest and endearing one that effectively bridges the gap between Maliza's childhood obstacles and her ultimate interest in research.

Maliza's essay is effective in providing insight into not only the obstacles she has faced but also the ways in which those obstacles have shaped her passions and worldview.

—Christina M. Teodorescu

YUEMING C.

My *Ye-Ye* always wears a red baseball cap. I think he likes the vivid color—bright and sanguine, like himself. When *Ye-Ye* came from China to visit us seven years ago, he brought his red cap with him and every night for six months, it sat on the stairway railing post of my house, waiting to be loyally placed back on *Ye-Ye*'s head the next morning. He wore the cap everywhere: around the house, where he performed magic tricks with it to make my little brother laugh; to the corner store, where he bought me popsicles before using his hat to wipe the beads of summer sweat off my neck. Today whenever I see a red hat, I think of my *Ye-Ye* and his baseball cap, and I smile.

Ye-Ye is the Mandarin word for "grandfather." My *Ye-Ye* is a simple, ordinary person—not rich, not "successful"—but he is my greatest source of inspiration and I idolize him. Of all the people I know, *Ye-Ye* has encountered the most hardship and of all the people I know, *Ye-Ye* is the most joyful. That these two aspects can coexist in one individual is, in my mind, truly remarkable.

Ye-Ye was an orphan. Both his parents died before he was six years old, leaving him and his older brother with no home and no family. When other children gathered to read around stoves at school, *Ye-Ye* and his brother walked in the bitter cold along railroad tracks, looking for used coal to sell. When other children ran home to loving parents, *Ye-Ye* and his brother walked along the streets looking for somewhere to sleep. Eight years later, *Ye-Ye* walked alone—his brother was dead.

Ye-Ye managed to survive, and in the meanwhile taught himself to read, write, and do arithmetic. Life was a blessing, he told those around him with a smile.

Years later, *Ye-Ye*'s job sent him to the Gobi Desert, where he and his fellow workers labored for twelve hours a day. The desert wind was merciless; it would snatch their tent in the middle of the night and leave them without supply the next morning. Every year, harsh weather took the lives of some fellow workers.

After eight years, *Ye-Ye* was transferred back to the city where his wife lay sick in bed. At the end of a twelve-hour workday, *Ye-Ye* took care of his sick wife and three young children. He sat with the children and told them about the wide, starry desert sky and mysterious desert lives. Life was a blessing, he told them with a smile.

But life was not easy; there was barely enough money to keep the family from starving. Yet, my dad and his sisters loved going with *Ye-Ye* to the market. He would buy them little luxuries that their mother would never indulge them in: a small bag of sunflower seeds for two cents, a candy each for three cents. Luxuries as they were, *Ye-Ye* bought them without hesitation. Anything that could put a smile on the children's faces and a skip in their steps was priceless.

Ye-Ye still goes to the market today. At the age of seventy-eight, he bikes several kilometers each week to buy bags of fresh fruits and vegetables, and then bikes home to share them with his neighbors. He keeps a small patch of strawberries and an apricot tree. When the fruit is ripe, he opens his gate and invites all the children in to pick and eat. He is *Ye-Ye* to every child in the neighborhood.

I had always thought that I was sensible and self-aware. But nothing has made me stare as hard in the mirror as I did after learning about the cruel past that *Ye-Ye* had suffered and the cheerful attitude he had kept throughout those years. I thought back to all the times when I had gotten upset. My mom forgot to pick me up from the bus station. My computer crashed the day before an assignment was due.

They seemed so trivial and childish, and I felt deeply ashamed of myself.

Now, whenever I encounter an obstacle that seems overwhelming, I think of *Ye-Ye*; I see him in his red baseball cap, smiling at me. Like a splash of cool water, his smile rouses me from grief, and reminds me how trivial my worries are and how generous life has been. Today I keep a red baseball cap at the railing post at home where *Ye-Ye* used to put his every night. Whenever I see the cap, I think of my *Ye-Ye*, smiling in his red baseball cap, and I smile. Yes, *Ye-Ye*. Life is a blessing.

REVIEW

Yueming quickly distinguishes herself with her refreshingly crisp writing. Avoiding a common pitfall in college application essays, Yueming uses the appropriate amount of descriptive language needed to illustrate her thoughts while keeping her prose clean and readable. She doesn't just use big words for the sake of using big words—a pitfall that many are aware of yet many still succumb.

In fact, her succinctness helps her essay shine. For example, the stark simplicity of the line "Eight years later, *Ye-Ye* walked alone—his brother was dead" makes it especially powerful. The sentence's abruptness hits the reader with the full force of the situation, unmitigated by secondary details. The terse, in-passing reference to *Ye-Ye*'s brother's death in itself is haunting, conveying a sense of coldness in the world that suits Yueming's intent perfectly.

Fundamentally, this reflects the underlying strength of this essay: Yueming's remarkable ability to tell a story. Her concise writing style lends itself well to this art, crafting a narrative that is evocative but easy to follow. Like many good storytellers, Yueming weaves recurring themes into her work, giving it a sense of unity. In particular, there is a persistent spark of optimism that her grandfather retains in the face of tremendous hardship, captured in the refrain, "Life was a blessing." It echoes throughout the piece, embodying the larger perspective of gratitude that Yueming credits to her grandfather. Inevitably, though, the heavy focus on her grandfather does come at the expense of her own story, as her role as an individual in the essay feels rather minor. As such, the reader doesn't learn enough about Yueming herself. Though she tells a compelling story, the reader comes away with a better understanding of *Ye-Ye* as a person than of Yueming.

But in spite of this flaw, the essay works. Yueming comes across as a compassionate individual with a talent for storytelling.

—Victor C. Wu

TONY CHEANG

Describe the world you come from—for example, your family, community or school—and tell us how your world has shaped your dreams and aspirations.

—Beauty in Complexity

Gazing up at the starry sky, I see Cygnus, Hercules, and Pisces, remnants of past cultures. I listen to waves crash on the beach, the forces of nature at work. Isn't it odd how stars are flaming spheres and electrical impulses make beings sentient? The very existence of our world is a wonder; what are the odds that this particular planet developed all the necessary components, parts that all work in unison, to support life? How do they interact? How did they come to be? I thought back to how my previously simplistic mind-set evolved this past year.

At Balboa, juniors and seniors join one of five small learning communities, which are integrated into the curriculum. Near the end of sophomore year, I ranked my choices: Law Academy first—it seemed the most prestigious—and WALC, the Wilderness Arts and Literacy Collaborative, fourth. So when I was sorted into WALC, I felt disappointed at the inflexibility of my schedule and bitter toward my classes. However, since students are required to wait at least a semester before switching pathways, I stayed in WALC. My experiences that semester began shifting my ambition-oriented paradigm to an interest-oriented one. I didn't switch out.

Beyond its integrated classes, WALC takes its students on trips to natural areas not only to build community among its students, but also to explore complex natural processes and humanity's role in them.

Piecing these lessons together, I create an image of our universe. I can visualize the carving of glacial valleys, the creation and gradation of mountains by uplift and weathering, and the transportation of nutrients to and from ecosystems by rivers and salmon. I see these forces on the surface of a tiny planet rotating on its axis and orbiting the sun, a gem in this vast universe. Through WALC, I have gained an intimate understanding of natural systems and an addiction to understanding the deep interconnections embedded in our cosmos.

Understanding a system's complex mechanics not only satisfies my curiosity, but also adds beauty to my world; my understanding of tectonic and gradational forces allows me to appreciate mountains and coastlines beyond aesthetics. By physically going to the place described in WALC's lessons, I have not only gained the tools to admire these systems, but have also learned to actually appreciate them. This creates a thirst to see more beauty in a world that's filled with poverty and violence, and a hunger for knowledge to satisfy that thirst. There are so many different systems to examine and dissect—science alone has universal, planetary, molecular, atomic, and subatomic scales to investigate. I hope to be able to find my interests by taking a variety of courses in college, and further humanity's understanding through research, so that all can derive a deeper appreciation for the complex systems that govern this universe.

REVIEW

On first read, this piece feels more like an advertisement for the Wilderness Arts and Literacy Collaborative than a personal statement. Tony dedicates most of his essay to detailing the lessons he learned from WALC, vividly describing everything from glacial valleys to salmon migration, instead of writing a truly personal narrative.

Inspiration

Tony does attempt to use his two-semester experience at WALC to trace the story of his personal development. Sometimes, his story comes through, to great effect—for example, Tony notes that although he initially hoped to attend the more "prestigious" Law Academy, he "didn't switch out" once he recognized the profound nature of his WALC experience. However, although he alludes to a change from his "previously simplistic mind-set," he doesn't really explain how his mind-set has transformed. Did WALC inspire Tony to pursue science research instead of law? If so, that would be a good thing to explicate.

Overall, this essay leaves the reader confused about its narrative direction. It would benefit from a stronger focus on a single story or narrative. Centering his essay on one particularly moving lesson or experience instead of his entire program would have allowed Tony to tell the story of his personal transformation in a more focused and engaging narrative.

But Tony does do an excellent job at demonstrating his remarkable ability to craft beautiful prose. Lines like that referencing his "thirst to see more beauty in a world that's filled with poverty and violence" are the highlight of the essay.

—Sandra Y. L. Korn

SIDARTHA JENA-SIDUJENA

As a child weaned on the biographies of Richard Feynman, Albert Einstein, and J. Robert Oppenheimer, I have always had an overwhelming awe for those individuals to whom brilliant scientific thought seemed to come naturally. I spent many childhood days poring over portraits of these great minds, brows furrowed, no doubt in the deepest of thoughts. However, as I read more and more about the scientists I worshiped, there was one image that repeated in nearly every textbook and biography: that of the Fifth Solvay Conference held in 1927 in Brussels, Belgium. The simple black-and-white photograph depicts some of the most revered names in physics and chemistry: Albert Einstein, Werner Heisenberg, Marie Curie, Niels Bohr, and many others, standing in three rows as a group of obedient schoolchildren would for a yearbook. Yet for all its simplicity, the image evokes in me an urge to become a part of the scientific community, perhaps more than any other prompt I can name. This Round Table of science, chivalrous in their passion for their fields of study and their noble quests for the secrets of the universe, inspire me not only for their individual accolades and discoveries, but also for their collaboration and their shared love for science. Whenever I saw the familiar black-and-white photo, I felt a renewed eagerness to pursue my own deeply founded interest in science, to share my findings with the world, and to meet and converse with those with similar ambitions and ideas. To be in the dynamic, intellectual environment of the Solvay Conference would be a dream come true, but I was about eighty years too late.

Ever since those childhood days, I have grown to apply my love for science both in and out of the classroom. Beginning with my love for

Inspiration

physics and growing into an equal appreciation for biology, chemistry, environmental science, and everything in between, I have taken every opportunity to pursue scientific exploration in all its forms. My extra reading on protein synthesis in my Honors Biology class in freshman year led to an independent project with a friend a few years later to determine a method for accurate protein tertiary structure prediction. My fascination with mechanics and the beauty with which the macroscopic world could be explained led to an equal fascination with the deviations from these rules that occur on the microscopic scale, and my independent study of quantum mechanics using a borrowed textbook from my physics teacher. Experiences out of the classroom also inspired me: I collaborated with an environmental society in Orissa, India, to publish an informational review of the state of freshwater resource management upon seeing the poor state of water utilization and management in many parts of the country. Inspired by the determination of many cancer survivors in my community, I accepted a role as Advocacy Chairman for my region's Relay for Life event with the hope to help further the quality of life for cancer survivors through research and education. Through my experience in advocacy I have come to learn that the power of hope, perseverance, and determination can often be just as healing and powerful as any medication.

Two of my most formative experiences during high school have been the Intel International Science and Engineering Fair, in which I participated in 2010 and 2011, and the Research Science Institute summer program, which I attended in 2011. The first time I attended the International Science and Engineering Fair (ISEF), I was blown away by the sheer magnitude of the event. Students from all corners of the globe, in a gigantic convention hall, and science projects as varied and diverse as the young scientists presenting them: everything from a miniature nuclear reactor to an eco-friendly design for a green roof. I was enthralled to find myself in the presence of high schoolers like me who wished to learn more and explore the world around them. This feeling continued when I was chosen to participate in the Research Science Institute (RSI) this summer, where I conducted research on gastric cancer development at Beth Israel Deaconess Medical Center while meeting some of the brightest science and mathematics students from all over the world. Some of my fondest memories are those of talking for hours on end with the other RSI students about our research and scientific interests, even gaining new ideas and ways of thinking and problem solving. These interactions made a lasting impression that will remain with me all my life.

The friends I made during my two years competing at ISEF and during the summer I spent at the RSI have stayed with me ever since, and I know that it is this group of students that will always strive to pursue the miracle cures, solve the food and water shortages in developing countries, help clean up our environment, and answer the most fundamental questions regarding our universe. I am honored and privileged to count myself as one of them. I have been fortunate to pursue many adventures in science, from the laboratory to the classroom to the community, but I have always loved more than anything else the feeling that I know I share with those who participated in the Solvay Conference: the atmosphere of being with peers who share the same passions as I do, pursue similar goals, and delight in the pleasure of learning. I can only dream of continuing this wonderful intellectual experience in my college studies, and in my journey through life.

REVIEW

Sidartha set out to write a beautifully constructed essay—a four-paragraph completed cycle, with a captivating introductory paragraph and a beautiful conclusion that ties the whole thing neatly together.

Inspiration

By reflecting on the collaborative nature of science, Sidartha inspires the reader to understand why science is so important to him; why his list of accomplishments is only because he is in love with the subject.

And while he opens strong, Sidartha loses quality in the second paragraph. Though he tries to insert some personality into a list of accomplishments, he's not tricking anyone. The 112-word paragraph adds very little that isn't included in other parts of his application, and bogs down an essay that has no need for it.

Sidartha gets back on track in his third paragraph, which also details his accomplishments, but with a focus on their effect on him. These "formative experiences" are the highlight of his essay, and what he should have focused on. When he focuses on himself as a person, rather than his accomplishments, Sidartha is successful.

Sidartha's mentions of the friends he has made while competing also serve to humanize an essay that otherwise focuses on accomplishments. This interaction with other students and scientists is interesting and unique, and complements the rest of his application perfectly. Drawing the focus to this, rather than the accomplishments themselves, would have made for a much better essay.

—Sara Kantor

VIII. EXPERIENCES

The most straightforward type of personal statement, essays on experiences rarely go wrong. The concrete nature of these essays leave little room for error, and everyone has some experience worth writing about. Telling a story is easier than explaining a source of inspiration or putting into words the goings-on in your head.

The most common mistake with these essays is when students take a perfectly good story and try to make it explicitly into a lesson. The best essays let the reader see the lesson you've taken from the experience, but don't require a literal statement. If you are thinking about concluding your essay with sentences like: "From _____ I learned . . ." or "_____ taught me how . . ." think again. This is a method that could work in very specific situations, but often, your essay would be stronger if you let the story speak for itself. If you have to put forward your meaning explicitly for the essay to make sense, then that is a good sign that there are places that need to be improved in your essay.

Remember, if you're writing an essay about experiences, use lots of detail and include some color. These stories should be told well enough that someone would want to read it even if they weren't being paid to do so.

CHARLES WONG

James was not fitting in with everyone else. During lunch, he sat alone, playing with his own toys. During group activities, the other campers always complained when paired with him. What was wrong? As camp counselor, I quietly observed his behavior—nothing out of the ordinary. I just couldn't fathom why the other campers treated him like a pariah.

After three days of ostracism, James broke down during a game of soccer. Tears streaming down his cheeks, he slumped off the field, head in his hands. I jogged toward him, my forehead creased with concern. Some campers loudly remarked, "Why is that creep crying?" Furious indignation leaped into my heart. They were the ones who "accidentally" bumped into him and called him "James the Freak." It was their cruelty that caused his meltdown, and now they were mocking him for it. I sharply told them to keep their thoughts to themselves. I squatted beside James and asked him what was wrong. Grunting, he turned his back to me. I had to stop his tears, had to make him feel comfortable. So for the next hour, I talked about everything a seven-year-old boy might find interesting, from sports to Transformers.

"I have a question," I asked as James began to warm to me. I took a deep breath and dove right into the problem. "Why do the other campers exclude you?" Hesitantly, he took off his shoes and socks, and pointed at his left foot. One, two, three . . . four. He had four toes. We had gone swimming two days before: All the campers must have noticed. I remembered my childhood, when even the smallest abnormality—a bad haircut, a missing tooth—could cause others, including myself, to shrink away. I finally understood.

But what could I do to help? I scoured my mind for the words to settle his demons. But nothing came to me. Impulsively, I hugged him—a gesture of intimacy we camp leaders were encouraged not to initiate, and an act I later discovered no friend had ever offered James before. Then, I put my hand on his shoulder and looked him straight in the eyes. I assured him that external features didn't matter, and that as long as he was friendly, people would eventually come around. I listed successful individuals who had not been hindered by their abnormalities. And finally, I told him he would always be my favorite camper, regardless of whether he had two, five, or a hundred toes.

On the last day of camp, I was jubilant—James was starting to fit in. Although the teasing had not completely disappeared, James was speaking up and making friends. And when, as we were saying our good-byes, James gave me one last hug and proclaimed that I was his "bestest friend in the whole wide world," my heart swelled up. From my campers, I learned that working with children is simply awesome. And from James, I learned that a little love truly goes a long way.

REVIEW

Although several high school students choose to draw from summer experiences to write their college essays, Charles writes a unique story that would definitely stand out from the crowd. Though the experience of working with a four-toed camper is a pretty unusual tale in itself, the true triumph of this essay comes from Charles's ability to depict his personality within those circumstances that could be quite jarring.

Charles's encounter with bullying is unique, but he tells the story with less sophistication than one would hope.

But this clear and straightforward tone also has its advantages. He tells his story in a simple, casual tone, unlike the formal voice high school students are *so* used to writing in essays and other papers. By doing so, the several sentimental moments in this essay, like the hugs or the pep talks, do not seem contrived. These actions truly seem like something Charles would do from the kindness of his heart. The most striking factor of this essay is not the unique tale, but the degree of success Charles was able to depict himself as a genuine and friendly person—someone Harvard or any college would love to have.

—Jiho Kang

LETITIA LI

The Very Essence of Fifth Grade

Blub. Piggypie. Pebbles.

It's nearly impossible to recognize the above words as names. And not just any names, but the names of the three most influential people of my life—my fifth-grade math team members and best friends.

For just their passing presence in my life, I consider myself eternally lucky. Our mutual love of experiencing life through our silly ways forged a friendship that has sustained and nurtured my individuality for all these years.

Welcome to my fifth-grade year.

Math competitions were exciting.

We had secret identities. On competition days, Melissa transformed into Blub, Joy morphed into Piggypie, Livvie reverted to Pebbles, and I embraced my alter ego, Yolanda. Despite being our elaborate attempt to intimidate all the other fifth-grade teams, we usually just ended up confusing ourselves.

We were fastidious in our traditions as a result of our combined idiosyncrasies. Our job responsibilities in the team rounds were even delineated down to specific problem numbers. Livvie cracked the tough even-evens (4, 8), Joy delved within the mysteries of the odd-evens (2, 6, and 10), Melissa outfoxed the tricky even-odds (3, 7), and I wrestled with the treacherous odd-odds (1, 5, and 9).

We made friends with our proctors. There was one in particular, "Princess Stone," who we thoroughly enjoyed. He proctored our very first competition, the "Math Is Cool" Invitational held at Mount Rainier

Experiences

High School, and we saw him year after year until our last, when we sadly learned he had graduated.

Outside of math, we were crazy.

We unofficially started the nature club. It didn't matter that it was just the four of us—it was awesome. One day at recess, we tasted purple flowers simply because Melissa was convinced they were edible. We didn't try that again. Edible they were; tasty they were not.

We started a class paper, filled with random occurrences, jokes, and useless anecdotes containing articles, such as, "How the Jaguar Got Its Spots," and distributed it to all our classmates and previous teachers.

We supported each other. When I was cast as Helena in our school play of *A Midsummer Night's Dream*, Melissa, Livvie, and Joy all showed up opening night to watch me interact awkwardly with my costar and onstage love interest, Demetrius.

We performed at our school's talent show. I had written a song in class called "Where Is Your Papa, Yolanda?" and choreographed a dance during recess. So while our classmates displayed their fine instrumental talents and sang Top 40 hits such as "Beautiful" and "Ain't No Mountain High Enough," we performed an interpretative dance to an original composition. We even recorded a background musical accompaniment on a cassette tape.

Fast-forward seven years.

My math trophies and ribbons are gathering dust in a closet I no longer visit. The tape recording of our interpretative dance has long disappeared and five editions of our newspaper sit in a dusty box with all my old classwork from my elementary days in Washington State. But the memories still linger, preserved pristinely in a capsule, ensconced within an atmosphere of lingering nostalgia.

I wish I could say we are still the closest of friends, but we're not. Distance and time are very real obstacles; however I'm convinced the feelings of acceptance and the lessons I've taken with me transcend those boundaries. Since then, I've heard Joy has gone on to excel in math at Exeter; Livvie has entered the University of Washington, skipping most of high school; and Melissa is following her ice-skating dreams.

And then there is me. Where am I and where will I go?

The inevitable passage of time is a great reminder that with all the change in the world, the exciting, smart, motivated person, whose friends helped her discover the courage to be different, is, amazingly enough, the person I am and still want to be.

Hence, I have continued embracing life and cherishing my unique personality in Indiana as a fulfillment of a past legacy of friendship and in honor of an incredible fifth-grade experience. So even though childhood is more forgiving of silliness, I am not ashamed of sharing those memories as a testament of where I came from and who I still am today.

So, yes, I am cocaptain of an internationally ranked color guard, and a glider pilot, and a tutor.

But I am also the same person who wrote a rap for a high school English performance; the person, who just last week, remarked that our drill formation looked like a phospholipid to a torrent of spastic laughter from fellow band geeks in my AP Biology class, and the person, who not long ago, loved performing interpretative dances, eating flowers, writing imaginative stories, and making math entertaining. (I still do.)

As for my future, I hope to carry on with my exuberance for life and learning. I aspire to meet wonderful people—the new Blubs, Piggypies, and Pebbles—to inspire and be inspired from. But most of all, I will strive to bring laughter and joy with me no matter where I go.

REVIEW

Letitia does a commendable job conveying her confidence in embracing a unique and quirky personality in this essay. The use of bizarre nicknames in the introduction is catchy, and the nicknames are only the first of many well-chosen details about the oddities of her and her math teammates' friendship. These details about the rituals and traditions of their group of friends do a brilliant job showing the eccentricities the essay is based upon.

The transitions through such large gaps in time and activities could present a challenge for a personal essay, given the limitations in length. However, Letitia orients readers nicely with framing sentences that divide the essay's sections. The best example of this is, "Fast-forward seven years," which concisely informs readers that time is moving. This is accompanied nicely with references to the trophies and other elements of the previous stories and where they are now, further orienting the reader.

Although the framing within the body of the essay is stellar, this author could continue to improve by setting up the essay's takeaway earlier on. Currently, readers aren't aware of what is at stake in the essay until the end thus making the essay slightly less satisfying as it could be.

Regardless, the essay illustrates a clear personality and confidence that would endear the author to any admissions officer.

—Juliet Nelson

Rory O'Reilly

Each tick pierced the cold November night; time was still moving—I could hear it—but the clock was surely destroyed.
Warped; slightly charred; hands stopped in perpetual stillness.

I looked away.

As glass slowly pierced the soles of my shoes, I stepped over our hardly recognizable delicacies: A Doritos bag—hot and spicy; a Fruit of the Loom T-shirt—once red, now black; a tear—slowly seeping into the carpet.

I looked at my mother, who was crying her heart out, and attempted to fathom what had just happened; the smoke had come out of nowhere. I didn't remember walking out of the house. I didn't remember pulling my brother out from his bed. I didn't remember grabbing our two cats and bringing them to the car. All I remembered was my father thrusting a jacket at me, and my mother placing shoes in my hands.

I looked back toward the clock. The hands were still stuck on 11:53.

Although the hands are stopped, the plastic is melted, and the numbers are disintegrating, the clock—at least to me—represents my own life. Time may have appeared to stop, but it didn't. It was the start of something better; it was the start of something brighter.

I realized that night that my time was just beginning. I needed to live every second to the fullest. I needed to live every minute like it was my last. Every month I needed to accomplish one of my goals; every year I needed to create new ones.

A fire was truly raging that night. The one in the house was bad, but it was nothing compared to the untamed one in my heart. No fire-fighter could ever put out my intensity. No extinguisher could stop me.

I snapped out of my trance, as wind brushed up against my bare legs; I did not have time to put on pants.

But I did have time. I had time to look at all of the little things I had lost in my life; but better yet, I had time to look at all of the little things I had kept. I glared at the burnt clock, and realized my life had changed.

It wasn't changed because I lost all my clothes.
It wasn't changed because I lost all my school books.
It wasn't changed because I lost my house.

It was changed because I had not lost myself.

REVIEW

In this succinct and memorable essay the author manages to communicate the passion for living life to the fullest.

The structure of the essay is particularly noteworthy. The small paragraphs separated by full line breaks and the use of poetic spacing emphasizing important lines make for a more dramatic read. What some might call a trivial choice, the unique spacing of the essay distinguishes it from the masses that admissions officers read and leaves a favorable impression.

Cohesion is another strength of this author. The seamless transitions between details of the fire and greater meaning taken from the event clearly conveying the author's ideas. The motif of the clock is a good example of this. A thread that appears throughout the essay, the clock gives a masterful sense of unity to the work. It first appears with melted hands as a detail of the aftermath of the fire but is then used to draw greater meaning when the author notes that time is continuing on despite the clock's stillness.

But even tragic events can be overdone, and Rory should have looked out for that. References to "the untamed [fire] in my heart" are too strong, and through hyperbole diminish the power of the story.

Overall, the essay is strong and clearly communicates the author's new intensity for life after the fire. The closing of the essay is particularly strong with its use of repetition. The author's juxtaposition of the items lost in the fire with the sense of purpose he now feels in the last lines of the essay emphasizes to readers what "things" he thinks are truly important.

—Juliet Nelson

LESLIE OJEABURU

Nerves of Steel

My bladder felt as though it would burst right out of my body and yet my mouth burned with an unquenchable thirst. I knew there could be only one grim and damp solution, but I could do nothing about it. I was stuck in a chair, awaiting my turn on the stage and my mind, body, and sanity were being held captive by my nerves. My legs were shaking as though I were in the snow with only my boxers on. My belly was in a Gordian knot and I could feel the telltale wetness that tends to form under my armpits in times like these. I was in no shape to give a speech to a room full of parents but there I was, violently clutching my papers at the side of the auditorium, awaiting my name to be called in a few seconds.

I took a deep breath. It wasn't as if this was my first time in front of a crowd. In fact, as student body president, I had gotten quite used to standing in front of hundreds of teens my age, giving announcements, transforming into Kanye West and President Obama in skits, and watching waves of laughter sweep through the entire room. Yet I knew this time it was very different. My audience was not filled with the young and often quick to laugh faces of teenagers but rather the hardened, mustached, and powdered ones of adults.

"Please welcome our student speaker . . . Leslie Ojeaburu . . . to the stage!" The voice jolted me from my thoughts and almost mechanically I rose from my chair. A huge awkward grin spread across my face as the sounds of Chopin's Funeral March echoed through my mind, but somehow I realized that I had to do what any good president would. I had to speak confidently and pray that no one notices the quaking of my hands.

Speaking has always been one of my favorite pastimes and each new speech I give . . . one of my greatest victories. You see my nerves, like that of many before me, are not made of steel. They buckle and scream under the assault of any strange, uncomfortable, or challenging moment in my life. Yet it was these very imperfections that forced me to work on public speaking, drove me to run for ASB offices, and taught me to throw myself headfirst into any situation that life may deal.

Indeed we all experience fears and anxieties in similar ways. We all have the same cold sweats, overactive bladders, and feelings of impending doom. Still, what truly distinguishes one from another is how fervently we embrace these fears as catalysts and not roadblocks to our goals.

I may not know where my public speaking will take me in life, but I do know that wherever I go my nerves will surely follow. Acting as constant reminders that there is always more I can improve on and always a new challenge waiting to be conquered.

REVIEW

It definitely takes guts to start a college essay by talking about your bladder. In the case of Leslie's essay, this risky move paid off: Personal statements without any foibles or humility read as unrealistic, unappealing ego boosts. Leslie's essay, on the other hand, most certainly does not portray its author as perfect, and by reveling in his own flaws instead of refusing to acknowledge them, the author evinces a charmingly self-effacing sense of humor, as well as a willingness to tackle challenges. Anyone who has ever delivered a speech with a quavering voice and a cold sweat running down their brow can easily relate to his detailed descriptions of his nervousness. Leslie does not try to cast himself as fearless, but rather as able to go on despite his fear—as a result, his essay has a sense of humor and believability.

But though he tells an interesting story, it leaves some questions unanswered. What is Leslie speaking about? Is the topic itself important, or is the experience his focus? Though he closes by explaining that overcoming this fear is his goal, the essay begs for answers to these questions and would be improved if he were able to deliver them.

Despite this blip, Leslie succeeds in crafting a winning personal statement that projects likability, determination, and ambition to overcome challenges to succeed, all without making Leslie come off as egotistical or cocky. His humorous and engaging essay serves its purpose well.

—Erica X. Eisen

ISAAC ALTER

Better Than Band Camp

"This one time, at flute camp—"

"Wait, what?"

Yes, I said flute camp.

It's a week in Carmel Valley, California, full of amazing and musically engaging experiences for middle and high school age flutists—

I sound like an advertisement. Let's try again.

It's the best week of my summer. Every year.

For one week every year, I get to spend all my time being an unrestrained flute nerd with awesome friends who are just as flute nerdy. (Or, if they're not, they won't judge me for being one.) Every single person there knows the Chaminade Concertino, a "flute anthem" that I could never discuss with any of my other friends without them looking at me like I was crazy.

At flute camp, we play hard and . . . play harder. We spend essentially all of our waking hours playing or practicing flute, watching performances, and listening to flute-related seminars. One such seminar was called "Tricks from Harry Flotter: Ridikkulus Scales!" Yeah, it's that cool. It sounds boring, but it literally never gets old, in part because I get to share all of it with some of my closest friends in the world. In addition to the scheduled activities, we always gather during our breaks to play card games (for years, we've been unable to stop playing "Five Crowns"), eat, or just talk about our lives (flutists tend to be drama queens, so this is always enjoyable). The isolated environment and our shared passion unite us and create lasting bonds; I stay in contact with my flute camp friends all year, no matter how far away they live.

Flute camp saved me. No, really. Before I first attended in 2009, playing the flute was an activity that was slowly drifting toward the periphery of my busy life; I practiced occasionally and indifferently. I left my first camp feeling more inspired than ever before—inspired to become a better musician and flutist, inspired to make flute a bigger part of my life. Hearing other flute players and learning about flute nonstop for a week straight always leave me with innumerable ideas about how to improve my own playing: What if I try out a faster vibrato like Catherine? How can I make my sound more like Noah's? In addition, the seminars about how to improve so many different aspects of flute playing always make me feel empowered, by giving me the will-power and the skills to take my playing up a notch (flute pun intended).

Now, playing the flute is my greatest extracurricular passion. It's quite literally an addiction. I need my flute "fix," or else I fall into periods of ennui and boredom with my school routine. Practicing flute is my way of de-stressing, of expressing myself, of having fun. There are simply not enough hours in the day for me to play flute as much as I want.

Flute camp taught me how to put my all into something I love, a lesson I have applied to all areas of my life; I now understand how to truly delve into a topic or an activity simply because it makes me happy.

That one time at flute camp changed my life.

REVIEW

A tongue-in-cheek tone is not a bad strategy for this kind of essay. He describes a relatively common experience (and one easily mocked) in a memorable way that also demonstrates his commitment and enthusiasm to that particular activity. The essay, and his personality as the flute kid, instantly stands out to the admissions committee. The defining levity of the piece also serves as a foil for the heartfelt and serious ending. He does not take himself too seriously but still appreciates the relatively serious lessons he has learned from the experience. Through humor, he essentially turns the potentially weak point of his essay into its strength.

Unfortunately, his attempts at humor overwhelm the essay to the point of distraction. Jokes that first present themselves as novel quickly become overdone. Isaac's essay would have significantly benefited from even a slight moderation in tone. His last two sentences are very good. They place the subject of his essay in relation to his individual personality very well and end on an inspirational note. He appreciates a particular opportunity and recognizes how it has changed him as a person. It's just that those two sentences are only two sentences. Had he limited his use of jokes more strategically and explained the significance of the experience earlier, it would be a truly great essay, a charming and heartfelt piece on the importance of finding and developing your passion.

—Raul P. Quintana

TARAS DRESZER

More Boluses to Dissect

Finally, I had found a volunteer opportunity at the Long Marine Lab, a marine biology research facility at UC Santa Cruz! I envisioned swimming with dolphins, or perhaps studying behavioral patterns of decorator crabs. But when I discovered the nature of my work on the first day of volunteering, my excitement turned to disappointment: I'd be picking through albatross boluses, the indigestible materials they cough up before going to sea. Sure enough, after three hours of separating fishing line from brown muck, I began to dread what I was in for. At that point, I had no clue of just how interesting the opportunity would turn out to be, and it would remind me of how easily I become engrossed and fascinated by all sorts of random stuff.

It didn't take long for my boredom with the boluses to shift toward curiosity. In the first place, the project itself was fascinating. The idea was to research the behavior and diet of albatrosses at sea. These birds can fly for months without touching land! When the birds have chicks, they cough up whatever they've eaten at sea to feed their young. When the chicks become old enough to fly, they cough up the hard, indigestible materials left in their stomachs. These boluses contain squid beaks that can reveal the types of squid eaten and the area where the squid were caught. We volunteers would pick through the boluses, separating out anything that looked interesting.

As I got better at dissecting these blobs, I started finding *crazy* stuff, and my colleagues and I would often discuss important findings. There was, of course, the search for the biggest squid beak, and the fish eyes were always interesting. But most shocking was the plastic. Beyond the normal Styrofoam and fishing line were plastic bottle caps, lighters, even toothbrushes. Occasionally, Asian writing revealed distant origins. Once, I picked through a bolus permeated with orange goo, eventually to discover the round mouthpiece of a balloon. The origins of these artifacts were sad, but also fascinating. I learned of the Texas-sized trash heap in the middle of the Pacific, the effects of which I was witnessing firsthand. I gained a heightened awareness of the damage inflicted on the oceans by humans, and their far-reaching impacts. Perhaps most importantly, I realized that even the most tedious things can blow my mind.

If dissecting boluses can be so interesting, imagine the things I've yet to discover! I play piano and can see myself dedicating my life to the instrument, but I can't bear to think of everything else I'd have to miss. I'd love to study albatrosses, but also particle physics or history, and preferably all three. At this point in my life, I can't imagine picking just one area. At the same time, though, I love studying subjects in depth. I tend to get overwhelmed by my options, since I can't possibly choose them all. But at least I know I'll never be bored in life: there are just too many subjects to learn about, books to read, pieces to play, albatrosses to save, and boluses to dissect.

REVIEW

Through the discussion of his unforeseen fascination with boluses, Taras shows how his experience of volunteering at a marine lab helped him not only to realize his interest in boluses, but also bolstered his intellectual curiosity. Consequently, the essay clearly and elegantly demonstrates Taras's drive to learn, which is one of the characteristics that admissions officers deem to be important.

Taras strays from his focus when he discusses the contents of the boluses—the essay is about his passion for research, not disservice done

Experiences

by humans to the environment. He successfully brings together a unique extracurricular activity—dissecting boluses—and his intellectual curiosity successfully. But attempts to tie in a passion for environmentalism as well fall short.

He successfully transitions from talking about boluses to elaborating on his diverse academic interests, which demonstrates his willingness to learn and be exposed to new environments.

—Jane Seo

LISA WANG

Playing It Dangerous

In hazy stillness, a sudden flurry of colored skirts, whispers of *"Merde!"* Sternly, my fingers smooth back my hair, although they know no loose strands will be found. My skin absorbs heat from stage lights above—if only that heat would seep into my brain, denature some proteins, and deactivate the neurons stressing me out. A warm hand, accompanied by an even warmer smile, interrupts my frenzied solitude. I glance up. My lovely teacher nods, coaxing my frozen lips into a thawed smile. A complex figure, filled in with doubt, yet finished with shades of confidence: My body takes its place and waits.

One, two, three, four; two, two, three, four. On stage, the lights and music wash over me. Never having had a true ballet solo before, my lungs are one breath away from hyperventilating. Trying to achieve a Zen-like state, I imagine a field of daisies, yet my palms continue sweating disobediently. It's not that I've never been on stage alone before; I've had plenty of piano recitals and competitions. Yet, while both performances consume my mind and soul, ballet demands complete commitment of my body.

Gently slide into arabesque and lean downward; try not to fall flat on face—Mom's videotaping. In terms of mentality, I would hardly be described as an introvert; yet, a fear of failure has still kept me from taking risks. Maybe I was scared of leaping too high, falling too far, and hitting the hard floor. As I moved up in the cutthroat world of dance, this fear only increased; the pressure of greater expectations and the specter of greater embarrassment had held me contained. Now, every single eyeball is on me.

Lean extra in this pirouette; it's more aesthetic. But is it always better to be safe than sorry? Glancing toward the wings, I see my teacher's wild gesticulations: *Stretch your arms out,* she seems to mime, *More!* A genuine smile replaces one of forced enthusiasm; alone on the stage, this is my chance to shine. I breathe in the movements, forget each individual step. More than just imagining, but finally experiencing the jubilation of the music, I allow my splits to stretch across the stage and my steps to extend longer and longer, until I'm no longer safe and my heart is racing. Exhilarated and scared in the best way, I throw myself into my jumps. I no longer need to imagine scenes to get in the mood; the emotions are twirling and leaping within me.

Reaching, stretching, grabbing, flinging . . . My fear no longer shields me. I find my old passion for ballet, and remember the grace and poise that can nevertheless convey every color of emotion. Playing it safe will leave me part of the backdrop; only by taking risks can I step into the limelight. Maybe I'll fall, but the rush is worth it. I'll captain an all-male science bowl team, run a marathon, audition for a musical, and embrace the physical and intellectual elation of taking risks.

REVIEW

Lisa dedicates the bulk of her essay to describing her first ballet solo and the life lessons learned during that experience. Making a single important moment into an applicable exemplar of important changes is a common tool for the personal statement and Lisa does it well. Her prose falls easily and gives the reader a solid feel for what Lisa might be like as a student and, more importantly, a person. Losing the "person" in a personal essay is a common mistake and attempting to highlight one's attributes can make an essay fall flat and toneless. Lisa avoids that well here.

Lisa masterfully hits many key moments in her personal statement.

Her opening blends art and science, subtly showing her depth as a student. The first two lines are excellent as the subject of dance immediately bumps heads with the language of science, allowing Lisa to hit one of the key purposes of a personal statement: demonstrating diversity. She successfully and humbly shows many different strengths using only one moment of her dance career.

The story's short length gives her room to finish the essay with a quick laundry list of things that she can conquer and presumably has. But this conclusion detracts significantly from her essay. Many of those things can be checked on a résumé by an admissions counselor. In an essay about taking risks, she plays it safe right at the end and stumbles just a bit. Overall, this is an excellent essay that would impress admissions officers at Harvard or any other college.

—Amy Friedman